MARY IN THE CHURCH

MARY IN THE CHURCH

Edited by
John Hyland, FMS

VERITAS
MARIST BROTHERS, ATHLONE

First published 1989 by
Veritas Publications
7-8 Lower Abbey St
Dublin 1
and
The Marist Brothers
Athlone

ISBN I 85390 043 5

Acknowledgements
The publishers are grateful to the following for permission to use copyright material: SPCK and the Catholic Truth Society for *The Final Report of the Anglican/Roman Catholic International Commission;* Fr Éamon Mac Craoidhe and Servite Publications for *Queen of the Bright Light;* Darton, Longman & Todd Ltd for *The Joy of All Creation: an Anglican meditation on the place of Mary* by Canon A.M. Allchin and for *The Blessed Virgin Mary* edited by H.S. Box and Eric Mascall; SPCK for *The Primitive Faith and Roman Catholic Developments* by Archbishop John Gregg; Seabury Press for *Portrait of a Woman* by Herbert O'Driscoll; Hodder & Stoughton Ltd and A.R. Mowbray & Co Ltd for *The Unutterable Beauty* by G.K. Studdert-Kennedy; Ecumenical Society of the Blessed Virgin Mary for the *ESBVM Newsletter;* Vita et Pax for 'Sensus Fidelium' in *One in Christ;* Marian Library, University of Dayton for *Marian Studies;* Michael Glazier Inc. and Dominican Publications for *Life in the Spirit and Mary* by Fr Chris O'Donnell; Allen Figgis & Co. Ltd for *Poems* edited by Austin Clarke; Desclée Editeurs for *Life of Father Champagnat* by Fr Marcellin Champagnat; William Heinemann Ltd for *Selected Poems* by Gerard Manley Hopkins; Irish Texts Society, c/o Royal Bank of Scotland, 22 Whitehall, London SW1A 2EB for *Early Irish Lyrics* by Gerard Murphy and *Aithdíoghluim Dána* and *Dán Dé* by L. McKenna and *The Poems of Blathmac, son of Cú Brettan, together with the Irish Gospel of Saint Thomas and a Poem on the Virgin Mary* edited by James Carney; Padri Maristi for *Origines Maristes* by J. Coste, SM and G. Lessard, SM and for *A Founder Speaks* by Fr Jean-Claude Colin; Verses from *The Jerusalem Bible*, published and copyright 1966, 1967 and 1968, and from *The New Jerusalem Bible* published and copyright by Darton, Longman & Todd Ltd and Doubleday & Co. Inc. are used by permission of the publishers; Bible text from the Revised Standard Version Bible, Catholic Edition, copyright 1965 and 1966 by the Division of Christian Education of the National Council of the Churches of Christ in the USA is used by permission; excerpts from the English translation of *The Roman Missal* © 1973, International Committee on English in the Liturgy, Inc. All rights reserved.

Cover design by Eddie McManus
Typesetting by Kairos, Maynooth
Printed in the Republic of Ireland by
The Leinster Leader Ltd

Dedicated to the memory of Eamon and Martin

CONTENTS

CONTRIBUTORS

Metropolitan Anthony Bloom, Metropolitan of Sourozh, is head of the Russian Orthodox Church in Britain.

Patricia Coyle lectures in Philosophy at Milltown Institute of Theology and Philosophy.

Cahal Daly, formerly of Queen's University, Belfast, was Bishop of Ardagh and Clonmacnois before returning to Belfast as Bishop of Down and Connor.

Donal Flanagan is an internationally renowned marian scholar and author of *In Praise of Mary* and *Theology of Mary.*

Romuald Gibson, a Marist Brother at present working in New Zealand, formerly taught at the Marist Brothers Second Novitiate in Fribourg, Switzerland. He is author of numerous articles on Marist history and spirituality.

John McHugh teaches in Ushaw College, Durham. He is a leading Scripture scholar and author of *The Mother of Jesus in the New Testament.*

Brian Magee, a Vincentian, lectures in Liturgy at Mater Dei Institute of Education.

Celine Mangan is a Dominican Sister who lectures in the Department of Semitic Languages at University College Dublin and at Milltown Institute of Theology and Philosophy in Dublin. She is a member of the Ballymascanlon Working Party and author of *Chronicles, Ezra* and *Nehemiah* in the 'Old Testament Message Series' edited by Michael Glazier.

Michael O'Carroll, Holy Ghost Father, is author of *Theotokos*, an encyclopedia of marian theology and devotion. He is Co-Chairman of the Ballymascanlon Working Party and Chairman of the Ecumenical Society of the Blessed Virgin Mary in Ireland and its founding inspiration here.

Christopher O'Donnell, a Carmelite, lectures in Systematic Theology at Milltown Institute of Theology and Philosophy in Dublin. He is author of *Life in the Spirit and Mary* and *At Worship with Mary*, as well as being a member of the Ballymascanlon Working Party which produced a document on devotion to Mary in the Catholic and Protestant Churches in Ireland.

Peter O'Dwyer, Carmelite, lectures at Milltown Institute of Theology and Philosophy and St Patrick's College, Maynooth. He is author of *Mary: a History of Devotion in Ireland.*

John Paterson, formerly Church of Ireland Dean of Kildare, is at present Dean of Christchurch in Dublin.

Alberic Stacpoole, a Benedictine monk of Ampleforth, is General Secretary of the Ecumenical Society of the Blessed Virgin Mary and editor of *Mary in Christian Dialogue.*

PREFACE

The publication of this volume, *Mary in the Church*, brings together the papers delivered at the National Congress on Mary in the Church Today which was held in Athlone in July 1984 to mark the centenary of the Marist Brothers coming to the town. The Brothers thought it appropriate that the past hundred years of their educational endeavours in the town and its hinterland should be celebrated by a congress honouring Mary, whose name they bear. Publication of the congress papers serves as a fitting commemorative tribute to the work of the Brothers in the Athlone area over the past one hundred years as well as bringing the fruits of the congress to a wider audience. It was indeed this concern to share the riches of the congress that served as a stimulus to publication in this year when the Marist Brothers celebrate the bicentenary of the birth of their founder, Blessed Marcellin Champagnat.

The congress week was one of thanksgiving celebration. The elements of prayer and reflection on the role of Mary in the Church today combined to make it an enriching and memorable experience for the participants, many of whom came from the wider Marist family. And all of this in the beautiful warm sunshine of that never to be forgotten glorious summer.

The congress was titled 'Mary in the Church Today'. It set out to examine from various perspectives the place of Mary in theology and her role in the Christian life. The Church with which we are most immediately concerned is the Irish Church and so it was to Irish theologians and mariologists that the congress organisers turned. This approach could be laid open to the limitations of insularity were it not for the inclusion of a number of non-native contributions as well as those from other Christian traditions. Our horizons were broadened and enriched through exposure to differing perspectives and traditions. The resultant varied combination was a multi-faceted overview of the scriptural, dogmatic, historical and devotional dimensions in mariology which form the basis of our Christian understanding of Mary. Conscious that a renewed understanding of Mary can benefit from the signs of the times, the valuable insights arising from the feminist perspective as well as the continuing ecumenical dimension were considered. The ecumenical sensitivity of the congress was clearly underlined in the contributions from the Anglican and Orthodox perspectives. Furthermore many of the contributors were members of the Ballymascanlon Working Party which in 1983 produced a document on devotion to Mary in the Church of Ireland, the Methodist Church in Ireland, the Presbyterian Church in Ireland and the Roman Catholic Church. Many were also involved in the Ecumenical Society of the Blessed Virgin Mary. Finally the Marist tradition of struggling to live in the spirit of Mary's *fiat* is shared, perhaps for the first time, with a wider audience.

The Marist Brothers are therefore pleased to be associated with Veritas in the publication of this volume. It is to be hoped that this book will be a worthwhile addition to the ongoing theological and devotional reflection on the role of Mary in the Church today.

In conclusion, the Marist Brothers acknowledge their indebtedness to Fr Chris O'Donnell, whose expertise was so willingly and generously shared both in the organisation of the congress itself and latterly in his gentle encouragement towards having this volume published.

John Hyland, FMS

1

MARY IN THE NEW TESTAMENT:
SOME THOUGHTS FOR TODAY

Reverend John McHugh

Our congress
The title of this congress is 'Mary in the Church Today', and every word in that title is important. A glance at the programme of lectures, or over the contents of this book, will quickly confirm that we are here to consider the role or function which Mary has within the Church Universal in our own day. It is legitimate, and very reasonable, to ask whether this role is any different from that ascribed to her one hundred years ago, when the Marist Brothers first came to Athlone; and, though in one sense her role remains, with that of her Son, Jesus Christ, the same "yesterday, today and for ever" (Heb 13:8), our appreciation of her position within the Church is not identical with what our forebears would have thought in 1884. And the reason is that we live in a different world from theirs, with different preoccupations, asking different questions from those which were predominant in 1884.

We live in an age of doubt and scepticism, especially with regard to religion and to many things which the Catholic Church teaches as dogmas of the faith. We live in a time when the Church is firmly committed to ecumenical activity; and many Catholics are not at all sure how much of the Church's traditional teaching, practices and devotions are of the essence of the faith. And even in Ireland, the major social or economic problem facing the Church is not the terrifying poverty of 1884, but a danger hitherto unknown here, the materialism of a consumer society. A congress concerned exclusively with Our Lady will not, of course, supply instant solutions for each and every one of these problems, but it has, I submit, more to offer to the contemporary world than might at first be thought. My own task is to speak about Mary in the New Testament, and I have selected three topics which will, I hope, be of some interest and assistance especially to those of you who are engaged in the instruction and education of the young. Today, fifty per cent of the population of the Republic is less than twenty-five years old, and the future of this country in the twenty-first century will very soon lie in their hands. In ten years from now it will be too late to teach them what they will need to know in order to deal with the problems of that new century; this task must begin now. And so I want to ask what has the picture of Mary in the New Testament to say *to us, today*, as a new, largely unknown, world is fast taking shape before our eyes.

I shall discuss three questions, each of which is of prime importance today, and about which there is, even among Catholics, some misunderstanding and even confusion: the virginal conception of Jesus, the perpetual virginity of his mother, and Our Lady's faith.

1. THE VIRGINAL CONCEPTION OF JESUS

The doctrine that Jesus was born of a virgin mother is stated both in the New Testament and in the most ancient creeds, and was until the beginning of this century regarded by almost all members of the major Christian Churches as a central dogma of the faith. Sad to say, this is no longer true today.

Some years ago, a most grave controversy was raging within the Church of England concerning the bishop-elect of Durham, who was due to be consecrated to that office by the Archbishop of York on Friday, 6 July 1984. In a television interview some weeks earlier, the then bishop-designate, Professor David Jenkins, stated that he personally did not think that Jesus was conceived of a virgin (though he would not exclude the possibility), and then added that he did not consider that the doctrine expressed in the creed necessarily involved acceptance of a biologically virginal conception as an historical fact. Similarly, he did not consider that belief in the resurrection of Jesus entailed belief in the raising to life of Jesus' material body; that too was not, in his opinion, an essential element of Christian faith in the resurrection.

We have all heard these views advanced before, but what was significant and disturbing about that particular controversy was that a number of bishops in the Church of England expressed sympathy, understanding or even agreement with the bishop-elect. He was in fact voicing, and without ambiguity, an opinion which is almost universally accepted among those who belong to the liberal Protestant tradition. It is no pleasure to add that in the last twenty-five years a number of Catholic writers have adopted exactly the same position; and one knows all too many young Catholics, untrained in theology, who take the same view purely on the authority of these writers, without ever examining the arguments on either side of the case.

In these circumstances, it seems rather pointless to argue from authority. It is certainly not much use appealing to the authority of the Church's traditional teaching, when it is precisely this traditional teaching which is being called into question. It is equally pointless to remind people that the overwhelming majority of Catholic theologians still firmly hold to the ancient tradition about Jesus' virginal conception; for what the young are asking is whether this view is right. So I am not going to argue from authority. Instead, I wish to examine carefully the reasons advanced for and against the traditional doctrine, and to ask which arguments are the more convincing when assessed in the light of the Christian faith as a whole.

And this can best be achieved by asking two separate questions:

(a)   Was Jesus in truth and in reality conceived without the intervention of a human father?
(b)   Does it matter?

The virginal conception: theological symbol or historical fact?
St Matthew (1:18-25) and St Luke (1:26-38) both relate the story of Jesus' virginal conception; but what do these stories really mean? The account of the creation of the world in six days (Gen 1) does not oblige us to believe that God created the world step by step in six twenty-four hour periods; nor are we expected to believe that the first woman was in reality shaped out of the first man's rib (Gen 2:24-25), or that in Noah's day a world-wide flood submerged Mount Everest (Gen 6-8). The

15

Bible does contain myths and legends, and no one can say *a priori* that the story of Jesus' virginal conception is not such a myth or legend.

For many centuries Christians used to believe that the Old Testament had predicted that the Messiah would be born of a virgin mother: was it not written in Isaiah 7:14, "Behold, the virgin shall conceive, and bear a son, and shall call his name Immanuel"? Those same Christians, believing that Jesus was in fact born of a virgin, regarded this fact as a proof that he was the expected Messiah, whose future coming had been foretold in the text just cited. This argument, however, can no longer be sustained. First, the Hebrew word used in Isaiah 7:14 does not denote one who is physically a virgin (Hebrew uses a different word for that), but simply a young woman of marriageable age. Secondly, the Jews certainly did not expect the Messiah to be born of a virgin — quite the contrary, as we shall see. The virginal birth of the Messiah was neither foretold in the Old Testament nor expected by the Jews.

One consequence of this is important. It has sometimes been said that the gospel writers made up the story of the virginal conception of Jesus in order to show that the prophecy of Isaiah had been fulfilled. But if Isaiah had never predicted a virginal conception, and if no Jew had ever suspected that he had done so, there was no point in making up such a story, for it would prove nothing to the Jews. All that St Matthew is doing when he quotes the text of Isaiah in 1:23 is asserting that, *given* the fact of the virginal conception of Jesus, it harmonises well with the Greek translation of Isaiah 7:14, where we do in fact read, "Behold, the *virgin* shall conceive. . .". But even here one must be cautious, for before the coming of Christ, no one had ever taken even this Greek version of Isaiah as predicting the virgin birth of the Messiah (since the Greek word too can also denote 'a young woman'). Consequently, it is most unlikely that the story of the virginal conception was simply "thought up" by the early Christians in order to prove to the Jews that Jesus was a virginally conceived Messiah, foretold in the Old Testament.

Others have suggested that the whole story is inspired by Greek mythology, which is full of legends about gods begetting children from human mothers. So the early Christians (they argue) made up this story to show to the pagan, Greek, world that Jesus was not in any way inferior to the Greek demi-gods, but was in his origins partly human and partly divine. Against this, it must be said that there is no parallel in Greek mythology to a *virginal* conception (there is always some physical contact between the Greek god and the human mother); and neither in Matthew nor in Luke is there even a hint that the Holy Spirit is in any way to be thought of as the (physical) father of Jesus. The account in the gospels is not about *pro*creation, but about direct *creation*. I mention this as a matter of largely historical interest, for nowadays almost no one would hold that the two gospel accounts, in the most Jewish and Palestinian sections of the gospels, are inspired by Greek or pagan mythology.

Today, the most common argument advanced against the historicity of the virginal conception is to say that it is a story made up by the early Christians to illustrate, in a profoundly beautiful and moving way, the truth that Jesus was in a totally unique manner the son of God. It is an eloquent, pictorial assertion of the doctrine of the Incarnation. That is what contemporary Christians like Dr Jenkins mean when they say that they accept and firmly believe the *truth* of the *doctrine* contained in the story ("that Jesus is in a unique manner God's Son"), but reject (or regard as of secondary importance) the idea that he had no human father. What are we to say of this interpretation?

There is, I think, one argument which tells decisively against accepting this view. If there is one thing certain from the Old Testament, it is that the Israelites most firmly believed that one day there would come a great deliverer, an anointed king or "Messiah", and that he would be *"of the seed of David"* (see 2 Sam 7:12; Ps 132:11.17; Is 11:1-3 etc.); and no future research is likely to overturn this statement. And if there is one thing certain from the New Testament, it is that the early Christians most firmly believed that Jesus of Nazareth was this promised Messiah; it was the principal name they gave to him — Jesus *the Christ*. Now if those early Christians had wanted to make up, for catechetical purposes, stories about his origin and birth, the obvious thing was to make up stories proving how he was truly descended, through his human father, from the seed of David. The last thing they would have been likely to think up was a tale that he had no human father at all, for that would be conclusive proof that he was *not* truly of the line of David, and therefore *not* the Messiah. The only factor which could possibly have induced them to affirm that he was conceived of a virgin mother was a firm conviction that everything had really so happened. And therefore we see, in Matthew 1: 18-25, the emphasis on the fact that Joseph took Jesus as his own son: what the evangelist is there saying is that, *in spite of* the virginal conception, Jesus was still truly of the line of David, because he was legally adopted by Joseph. In short, it seems to me inconceivable that the early Christians would have made up *this* particular story denying to Jesus any human paternity unless they had been solidly convinced that the fact was so.

The virginal conception: its doctrinal significance

But does it matter? It is sometimes said that the Second Person of the Holy Trinity, in taking to himself a human body and soul, could not have had a human father. This is a very feeble and foolish argument, for if it were valid, it would equally prove that he could not have had a human mother; and in any case, it sets bounds upon God's omnipotence, which is logically absurd. We must therefore begin by asserting unambiguously that the Second Person of the Holy Trinity could, had he so willed, have become incarnate in a human body conceived in the normal way, through sexual intercourse.

If that is so, then we have to inquire very carefully why, according to the Catholic and Orthodox tradition, the doctrine of Jesus' virginal conception is put forward as of such prime importance. And it is a real pleasure to affirm that the finest exposition of its relevance and significance known to me is to be found in the work of that giant among Protestant theologians of our day, Karl Barth. Here is one point upon which authentic Catholic, authentic Orthodox and authentic Protestant tradition can unite to speak with one voice.

In the Apostles' Creed we assert that Jesus was "conceived of the Holy Spirit, born of the Virgin Mary". In these two phrases, three statements are made.

"He was conceived of the Holy Spirit". That is, the origin of Jesus' human body is wholly and entirely the work of the Holy Spirit, of him whom we call the *Creator Spiritus*. Its origin owes nothing to the active intervention of any man; the body which wrought our redemption upon the bitter cross came into existence only by the direct intervention of God, not by human procreation, but by direct creation. That is the main point of the doctrine, and of the first assertion in the creed: "he was conceived of the Holy Spirit".

But there is in the creed a second phrase: "born of the Virgin Mary". Whereas the first phrase asserts God's role in the Incarnation, this second phrase defines the part played by humanity in the mystery, and it contains two statements, which are logically best expressed in the order of the Latin text: *natus ex Maria virgine.*

"*Natus ex Maria*" — "born of Mary". It is in the first place an affirmation that Jesus is truly man, truly and really born of a human mother, as much a member of our race as any other son or daughter of a human mother. His human body was directly created by the Holy Spirit of God, certainly; yet it was not created out of nothing, *ex nihilo,* but out of the flesh and blood of his mother. So the second affirmation of the creed is that the body which was directly created by God is also physically related to our race. He is one of us.

But the creed does not stop there: it adds, "of Mary *the Virgin*" —"*ex Maria virgine*". The reason for the mention of Mary's virginity is to assert that the role played by the human race in the Incarnation is simply that of accepting God's gift as a gift and as a grace, and nothing more. It is a firm denial that, apart from Jesus, mankind made any *active* contribution to its own redemption. Whenever we say "born of Mary *the virgin*" we solemnly affirm that humanity's part in the work of redemption lay solely in freely accepting salvation from the hand of the Omnipotent: "Behold the handmaid of the Lord! Be it done unto me according to thy word!" (*Lk 1:38*)

Thus the first and fundamental point of the doctrine of the virginal conception is to affirm that the human body and soul of Jesus is *a new creation*; that is why we call him the New, or the Second, Adam.

And from this there follows a second, consequential, truth. Where every other human being except Mary, his mother, failed to live out fully a life of complete obedience to God, the man Jesus of Nazareth, our brother, flesh of our flesh, achieved this. He lived through infancy and boyhood, through adolescence and manhood, in perfect obedience to the Father, even unto death; and thereby, as man, redeemed us all. Newman has expressed it perfectly:

> O loving wisdom of our God!
> When all was sin and shame,
> A second Adam to the fight
> And to the rescue came.
>
> O wisest love! That flesh and blood
> Which did in Adam fail,
> Should strive afresh against their foe,
> Should strive and should prevail!

And there is yet a third truth logically linked with those first two doctrines. That same body, born of Mary, crucified for our salvation, precisely because it was "conceived of the Holy Spirit" and was thereby God's new creation, was for our sakes raised from the tomb and taken out of earthly space and time into a new world — removed, as it were, out of our three-dimensional universe into a kind of fourth dimension, which we may call the "resurrection-world". There Jesus lives eternally, glorified in his humanity; and that human body, virgin-born, crucified, now glorified, is the first cell of the new world of the resurrection, from which we shall one day receive our own, glorified, bodies.

At the very basis of this vision of the New Creation stands the Church's teaching that the body of Jesus was in truth and in reality formed by the Holy Spirit in the womb of a virgin. That teaching is an affirmation that mankind contributed nothing to this work of redemption and re-creation, except in Jesus Christ, who achieved it all. The only thing that we poor creatures could do was freely, humbly and gratefully to accept this gift of salvation from the hand of God; and this was done first and principally by Mary.

All these ideas are involved in, and implied in, the Catholic doctrine of the virginal conception, which is anything but a bald statement of a miraculous exception to the laws of biology. The question of whether in reality God's New Creation has already come into being, did in fact start almost two thousand years ago, in Galilee. That is why every candidate for baptism is required to profess belief in this doctrine; and in confessing this faith, he also says in effect of the Incarnation and of the Redemption, "To God alone be glory!"

St Augustine puts it well: "Let all human merits here fade into silence, for they came to an end through Adam, and let the grace of God hold sway (as it always does), through Jesus Christ our Lord, the one and only Son of God, the one and only Lord" (*De praedestinatione sanctorum* 15, 31 — Pl 44:983).

II. MARY'S LIFE-LONG VIRGINITY

"Ever-virgin" is one of the most ancient titles given to Mary, and her life-long virginity is still taught by the Catholic and Orthodox Churches as a most important article of the faith. Yet outside the Catholic or Orthodox Communion, it is regarded as almost a mark of eccentricity to suggest that Mary did not have children other than Jesus. Once again we must ask whether she really did remain a virgin to the end of her life, and whether it matters. As in the previous lecture, and for the same reasons, I do not wish to appeal to any argument from authority, either ecclesial or scholarly, but simply to examine the evidence.

The brothers of Jesus
A number of New Testament texts mention certain "brothers of Jesus"(for example Mk 3:31-35); indeed, some mention sisters too (Mk 6:3 and Mt 13:55-56), though no sister is ever mentioned by name. The question is, were these individuals children of Mary? From around AD 380-400, three answers have been given to this question.

The first answer, which is nowadays held by almost all members of the Reformed tradition, is that these individuals were in fact blood-brothers of Jesus, sons born to Mary and Joseph after the birth of Jesus (and this position is equally common among many who would strongly affirm that Jesus himself was virginally conceived). The weakness of this view is that according to Mark 15:40 and the parallel text in Matthew

21

27:56, among the women who witnessed the death of Jesus was "Mary the mother of James the little and of Joses". The same "Mary the mother of James" was also one of the women who discovered the empty tomb (Mk 16:1). Now it is surely inconceivable that St Mark would, at this point of the story, have referred to the mother of Jesus in this curious and roundabout way. The only other occasion on which a certain James and Joses are mentioned in Mark is at 6:3, where Jesus is said to be "a brother" of theirs. Taken on its own, Mark 6:3 would most naturally imply that Jesus, James and Joses were blood-brothers; but when 6:3 is taken together with 15:40, we must surely look for another explanation, for "Mary the mother of James and Joses" is clearly not Mary, the mother of Jesus.

The second explanation is that favoured in the Orthodox Churches. According to them, the "brothers of Jesus" were children of Joseph, born of a previous marriage (and therefore older than Jesus). The objection to this view is that this is certainly not the impression given by the gospels, and (more importantly) that when Jesus is called *Mary's* first-born son (Lk 2:7), it seems to be taken for granted that he was also the first-born heir of Joseph (cf. Mt 1:18-25).

Hence the Western, Latin Church has, since the time of St Jerome, adopted a third view, namely, that the brothers of Jesus were in fact first cousins, and only called brothers in a wide sense (as in some texts of the Old Testament, and in many African societies today). This view is popular because at first hearing, it seems to safeguard the life-long virginity of Mary and to provide a suitable, not far-fetched, meaning for the term "brothers".

But this too is unacceptable, for reasons which non-Catholic scholars are not slow to point out. Firstly, St Jerome's theory is that Mary the mother of James and Joses was the *sister* of the Blessed Virgin (cf. Jn 19:25); is it likely that two sisters were each called Mary? Secondly, whatever may be said of Hebrew usage in the Old Testament, the New Testament was written in Greek; and Greek has a perfectly good word for "cousin" (*anepsios*, used in Colossians 4:10).

Hence I suggest a fourth interpretation, which I think does justice to all the texts. Suppose that Mary the mother of James and Joses was the sister, not of the Blessed Virgin, but of

Joseph; the first objection to St Jerome's theory falls to the ground. Suppose, secondly, *either* that this Mary, the mother of James, lost her husband, and then went to live in the same house as her brother Joseph, *or* that after the death of Joseph, the Blessed Virgin went to live with her sister-in-law. Jesus, James and Joses (though in fact first cousins) would then have lived (perhaps even grown up) as foster-brothers. There is much more that could be said on this topic, but this interpretation does, I think, make sense of the gospel texts, and there is much evidence for it in early patristic literature, which we cannot discuss now. Yet it is not the end of the problem we are dealing with in this lecture, for even if the brothers (and sisters) of Jesus were not children of Mary and Joseph, and even if Jesus (virginally conceived) was their only child, this does not prove that Mary and Joseph lived out their married life in virginity. To this we must now turn.

The marriage of Mary and Joseph
In St Luke's story of the Annunciation, we read that when the angel told Mary she was to bear a son, Mary replied "How shall this be, since I know not man?" It has often been held that by these words Mary was saying that she had taken a vow, or made a resolution, to remain a virgin all her life, and this interpretation has been so constantly preached that most Catholics probably simply take it for granted.

Yet there are two great difficulties against it. (1) Was it likely that a Jewish girl, in her culture and society, would ever make such a resolution? (2) If she did, was not her forthcoming marriage to Joseph thereby rendered null and void? One could perhaps answer the first objection by saying that one cannot judge Mary by ordinary standards (particularly in view of her Immaculate Conception); but this still leaves the second difficulty untouched and unanswered (and it was an objection that the great medieval theologians felt most keenly). Indeed, we may add that even if she had made such a vow, this does not of itself prove that she remained a virgin all her life, for one would have to prove that she never retracted it, and always kept it.

But there is another way of approaching this text, which is universally accepted today by all Catholic scholars. Luke's story of the Annunciation is not to be thought of as a transcript of a conversation between Mary and an angel, such as might have been taken down in short-hand or recorded on a cassette by an observer, had one been present. Rather, it is Luke's way of presenting in story the *fact* of Jesus' virginal conception. And into this story, he has introduced another assertion. By placing upon Mary's lips the words "How shall this be, since I know not man?", he is asserting *not* that Mary at that moment before the Incarnation had already made a resolution to remain a virgin for ever, but that she had in fact been *destined* to remain a virgin all her life. In short, Luke (writing probably between AD 70 and 80) is here implicitly affirming that Mary *in fact* remained a virgin all her life.

On this interpretation, it is quite possible to hold that Mary at first contemplated a normal marriage with Joseph, and chose a life of virginity only after, and in consequence of, her virginal conception. If this is true, then the two objections mentioned in the last paragraph but one no longer hold: the first simply disappears, and the second becomes irrelevant if Mary and Joseph agreed to live together, but in continence, in order to serve this miraculously conceived child.

This — admittedly new — interpretation is in complete harmony with Catholic doctrine, but it does entail a radical rethinking of what is involved in the concept of Mary's life-long virginity. And I suggest that this new interpretation has a very profound message of pastoral importance for the Catholic Church today.

The religious significance of Mary's life-long virginity

For a thousand years Catholic exegetes and theologians and preachers have explained that Mary had made a resolution of virginity before the Annunciation, and on the basis of this interpretation they have enriched the Church with much fruitful and constructive thought concerning the value of virginity consecrated to God.

On the other hand, this theology and these sermons have not contributed much to a deeper understanding of the sacrament of marriage, for they can all too easily convey the impression that virginity is something good in itself, irrespective of the motive for which it is chosen, as if the value of virginity lay in its purely negative aspect of abstaining from sexual pleasure. Not all preachers have avoided this danger, but the proposition is frankly Manichaean, and a blasphemy against him who created and ordained the use of sex, who made mankind male and female (Gen 1:27) and pronounced that "It is not good for a man to be alone" (*Gen 2:18*).

But if we assume that until the moment of the Incarnation both Mary and Joseph intended to consummate their marriage, and that they changed their plan after it, a far richer theology of marriage and of virginity emerges.

First, the holiness of the physical union between man and wife is proclaimed for all time, and in conjunction with the central mystery of the Incarnation. For the Word of God then chose to be born of a woman who was aspiring to serve God through marriage; and Catholics will add that this woman, who was conceived without trace of original sin, had at first every intention of living a normal married life. There is thus no place for a Manichaean attitude to sex within the framework of this theology.

Secondly, the still higher value of a love transcending sex is also demonstrated. No Christian (indeed, no sensible pagan) will pretend that the supreme good of marriage is to be sought or found in the physical pleasure of sexual union; all will agree that the greatest thing in marriage consists in the deep personal spiritual love of which physical endearments are but the imperfect expression and the sign, so that the greater love is often to be seen in illness, in suffering, and at the approach of death. Mary and Joseph, by their embracing of virginity, call attention to the primacy of this greater love. By their first intention of consummating the marriage, the positive religious value of physical love is set before the world for ever; by their subsequent choice of virginity in order to serve Jesus, a still nobler and wholly unselfish love is made known.

Thirdly, Mary and Joseph are more clearly seen as models for all Christian parents, whose love for their children so often demands immeasurable self-sacrifice, and a dying to oneself. By their agreement to devote their lives totally to Jesus, "their" son, Mary and Joseph show how the mutual love of husband and wife may be expressed and deepened through the love of God and one's children, so that those who lose their life in this way truly find it (Lk 9:24).

Fourthly, a much sharper picture of what is involved in *Christian* virginity emerges. In many non-Christian religions, abstinence from sex is esteemed purely because it is evidence of great self-control, of the dominance of the spirit over the flesh. But in the Jewish and Christian tradition, the flesh is just as holy as the spirit, and the worst sins are those of the soul, like hatred and pride. In the Christian tradition, the motive for choosing virginity must be not negative but positive, namely, to dedicate oneself completely and unconditionally to the service of God and one's fellow-men, irrevocably, for the whole of one's life, in the name of Jesus. And if it was after, not before, the Incarnation that Mary and Joseph decided together on a life of virginity, then they were the first ever so to dedicate themselves to virginity *in the name of Jesus.*

When we put all these four points together — about husband and wife, about parents, about consecrated virginity — we find that a constant theme runs through them all. For each of these four points is a reminder to the world that there is one thing only which matters: all things pass away, except charity (1 Cor 13).

III. MARY'S FAITH

Our third and last biblical topic is Mary's faith, and it too will be treated in three sections. There is indeed a text from St Mark (Mk 3:20-21, 31-35) which ought also to be discussed; but it is a difficult and complex text, to which one could not do justice in the time at our disposal. So for this text, may I simply refer you to the books mentioned at the end of this chapter, while forewarning you that the conclusions put forward in the North American work, *Mary in the New Testament* are very different from those set out in my own book.

At the Annunciation
St Luke's account of the Annunciation (Lk 1:26-38) is not to be read as a verbatim transcript of a conversation between Mary and an angel, but as the evangelist's way of expressing in story the doctrine that Jesus came into this world by a virginal

conception. The main thrust of the narrative is, as we have seen, christological; but it also tells us something about Mary.

Both Matthew (1:18) and Luke (1:27) state that the conception of Jesus took place at a time when his mother, Mary, was betrothed to Joseph. The fact is important, for it is undisputed that the normal age for betrothal was (for the girl) between the age of twelve and twelve and a half years, with the marriage following about one year later. So we should think of Mary as being at the time a young girl who had just reached puberty.

What, then, are we to make of the story of the Annunciation? Or (as it is sometimes rather crudely expressed) did it really happen? Obviously, it would be logically absurd to say that there *could not* have been an angelic apparition, for that is implicitly to deny God's omnipotence. Equally, one cannot say that Gabriel *did not* appear, for that also is to imply that one has certain, personal, knowledge of what exactly did happen. But we must also beware of going to the other extreme, by affirming that there certainly was, and must have been, an angelic apparition; for that also is to claim that one has absolutely certain knowledge of what happened. Yet both in the Old and in the New Testament we are generally dealing with writings which follow strictly Jewish conventions; and one of the most regular of these conventions is that when an author wishes to say that "God spoke to a man", he writes (in order to preserve the distance and transcendence of the Godhead) "God sent an angel to say. . .". So there is no reason why a Catholic should not hold that all Luke means by this story of the Annunciation is that Mary freely consented to God's plan, by which she became the virgin mother of Jesus.

In that case, what exactly happened? I would suggest that Mary, at the time when she was just betrothed to Joseph, had a mystical experience: by this, I mean a clear and unmistakable awareness of a message from God in her soul. In her case, it was a question: "Are you prepared to do anything, without reservation, however unlikely or impossible, that is to be asked of you?" And Mary said "Behold the handmaid of the Lord!" And then, while still a virgin, she discovered that she was going to have a baby.

This interpretation is in no way contrary to Catholic

doctrine or theology. Indeed, it breathes the spirit of Catholicism far more clearly than the usual, more fundamentalist, interpretation of the scene. For on the usual interpretation, Gabriel first reassures Mary that there is nothing to fear; then tells her that she is going to have a son; then, in response to her query, explains that he will be conceived by the power of the Holy Spirit (and therefore will be called God's son); and finally offers supplementary proof of the event by telling her of Elizabeth's conception. And only then does Mary say "Behold the handmaid of the Lord!" On the interpretation I have proposed, Mary simply puts herself into the hand of God, leaving all the future in his care.

At Cana

We turn now to the Gospel according to St John, where the mother of Jesus is mentioned twice, once at the beginning and once at the end, at Cana and on Calvary. In neither place is she named; both texts speak of her only in relation to her son — for John, she is simply "the mother of Jesus".

The Cana episode is particularly complex, and so I want merely to state, without proof, what I consider the most probable meaning of the text, insofar as it concerns the mother of Jesus. The story ends with the words: "This, the beginning of signs, Jesus did at Cana in Galilee, and manifested his glory; and his disciples believed in him" (*Jn 2:11*).

The message of that verse is clear: it was after this sign, and as a result of it, that the disciples who had in chapter one seen him as Messiah and so forth, began to *believe* in him: that is, to trust in him as being what he claimed to be. But in chapter 2:1, "the mother of Jesus" is distinguished from the disciples (who are first mentioned here in verse 2); and in verse 5 she says to the servants, "Do whatever he tells you!" These are the crucial words. Before Jesus has worked a single sign, before the disciples have begun to believe, the mother of Jesus has total faith in him, so that she can say, "Do whatever he tells you!" (Note that this would harmonise perfectly with the interpretation just given of Mary's response at the Annunciation.)

But what of chapter 2:4, where Jesus says, "Woman, what is that to me and to thee? My hour is not yet come". His mother calls his attention to the shortage of wine at the wedding feast, and Jesus replies, "Of what concern is that to you, or to me?" This is merely an earthly mishap, a sad and disappointing embarrassment, but of no real concern to Jesus or his mother. Both for Jesus and for his mother, far greater trials and sufferings lie ahead, though that hour is not yet come.

But this most important point once made, the story can proceed, with the command to the servants, "Do whatever he tells you!" And the evangelist's point is made, right at the beginning of his gospel: before Jesus had worked a single sign, his mother believed in him, totally.

On Calvary
We meet her next at the very end of St John's Gospel (19:25-27), where we read "There stood by the cross of Jesus his mother...". There she is presented to the disciple whom Jesus loved as his mother, and he is presented to her as her son. What is the doctrinal message contained in this text?

"Woman, behold thy son!" By addressing Mary not as "Mother" but as "Woman", Jesus draws attention away from his own blood-relationship with Mary, to focus attention on her as an individual, whose faith has endured to the end. Similarly with the beloved disciple, whose faith has also endured to Calvary. The disciple who stood by the cross is a type of all whom Jesus loves, and whose faith perseveres; but in the light of John 2:11, we should say that his faith (great as it was) had been founded on signs. He is summoned to look upon Mary as his mother, she to look upon him as her son.

For St John, it is the mother of Jesus who is the prototype and exemplar of faith, and that is why she stands at the beginning and at the end of St John's Gospel. She is there at Cana, fully believing, before Jesus has worked a single sign; and she is present beside the Crucified, when all the signs and wonders of the past appear to have been but a snare and a delusion. Where were those who had come to believe in Jesus because he had raised Lazarus from the dead? Had they perhaps ceased to believe, convinced there was one thing he could not do — bring himself to life again when dead — never suspecting that even at that fateful hour he was still keeping the best wine till the last?

29

But Mary's faith in her son had never been founded on the evidence of astounding miracles, only on complete trust in the mysterious ways of God. That is why it survived even on Calvary, neither looking for nor expecting any visible wonder, but quietly content to "do whatever he might tell her". That is why Mary, as she stands beside the Crucified, is there commended by the Word Incarnate to all his disciples, to be from that time forward their model and their mother. The portrait of the mother of Jesus in St John is meant to show all future ages what faith really involves, so that when all hope is lost, and evil triumphant, we may still be found beside the Crucified, still enduring, still believing that "nothing is impossible to God" (*Lk 1:37*). For to Mary above all others applies the beatitude with which the fourth gospel closes: "Blessed are those who have not seen, and yet have believed" (*Jn 20:29*).

2

GROWTH AND DECLINE IN MARIOLOGY

Christopher O'Donnell, O Carm

There is no such thing as purely objective history. Historians are always people of their time, formed by their culture, dominated by their own interests, selective in what they record, their very judgement of what is significant being itself an interpretation. The historian of mariology is no different. As we examine two millennia of theology and devotion to Mary, we approach these from our standpoint. The task is not made easier by the sheer scope of our subject. The history of mariology is found in theological documents, in devotional forms, in paintings, icons, architecture, sculpture, in religious and secular literature, especially poetry. All of these forms have their own criteria which must be respected if we are to reach the truth which they enshrine: the *Akathistos* hymn cannot be read as if it were a theological treatise; medieval stained glass cannot be interpreted the same way as eastern icons or Italian Renaissance paintings. Furthermore, we are in the end dealing with the one whose role in the eternal plan of God will always remain a mystery beyond human understanding.

As living realities, devotion and theology of Mary will have times of growth and decline. Here already we have a problem, for how do we decide what is growth and what is decline? The analogy from life is perhaps the most helpful. If we look at a tree we see what might have become strong branches, but did not, the direction the trunk might have taken, branches that regularly bear green leaves, dead branches that will never produce foliage again, off-shoots that do not enhance the central configuration of the tree. When we survey a vast subject like mariology and look for growth and decline, we are making judgements about what advanced, what bore fruit, what flourished for a time only, what were odd off-shoots. We can be neither comprehensive given the scope of the topic, nor objective given the nature of history. What we present is an interpretative overview of some periods of the history of mariology from the standpoint of the post Vatican II period. The value such an investigation might have is not simply historical: it is looking at the past, so that we might derive some guidance for the present.

There will be a very obvious contention in this overview, namely, that mariology is never abstract, but rooted in theological and secular cultures, and in turn reflecting them. More significant is the theological and historical judgement that there are three axes of mariology. When these are in harmony, there has been growth; when they are not balanced, or any one is neglected, there has been decline. The three axes, or overmastering norms, are Mary's relationship with her son and his mission, Mary's relationship with us, and finally the beauty of Mary. Thus, as we shall see, there were times when Mary's relationship with us was presented in a way that did not harmonise with the truth about her relationship with her son's mission; there were other times when there was some theological accuracy about her role in the salvific plan of God, but a failure to appreciate the beauty of the virgin; there were, too, times when there was focus on the glories of Mary that detracted from her son.

We will consider briefly five periods of the history of theology dwelling in a little more detail on the past four decades. It will, I hope, emerge that mariology is conditioned always by theological and secular culture. The periods which we select also show, for the most part, a harmonious balance of the three principles of Mary's beauty seen in relation to her son and to the Church.

The first period is from the second to the seventh century and it will be covered in more detail in another paper of this congress. The key issue that arose as soon as Christianity gained theological and psychological independence from narrow Judaism concerned Christ: who and what was he, what did his mission accomplish for us? Many quite crucial matters were involved in these apparently simple questions: there are trinitarian issues about the relationship of Father and the Son; there are christological difficulties as the Church sought to clarify what the assertion means, that God became truly man; there are controversies about grace and how we come to holiness through the merits of Christ. The world culture was still Greek with a desire for intellectual order and precision. The theological culture was scriptural and the Church pondered God's word for solutions to the problems which arose.

In this period reflection on Christ as the New Adam gave rise to the figure of Mary as the New Eve associated with the saving work of her son. The dominant reaction of the believer before the New Eve was thankfulness to God for this merciful plan and a sense of the wonder of it all. None was more eloquent than the Syrian, St Ephraem (d. 373), from whom we cite a random section of a sermon:

> Mary can most fittingly be given many names. She is the temple of the Son of God, who entered the holy place quite differently than the way he emerged: he came to her womb without a body, he came forth from her womb in a body of flesh. She is that mystical new Heaven in which the King of Kings had his throne and from which he glided down to this earth. . . . In the beginning the world was created, today it is renewed; in the beginning the crime of Adam resulted in the world being cursed in its work; today peace and security are restored to the world. In the beginning death was passed on to humanity through the sin of our first parents; today because of Mary we are transferred from death to life. In the beginning the serpent seized the ear of Eve and poison spread to the whole body of humanity; today Mary's ears accept the declaration of perpetual happiness.[1]

In this period too her virginity was seen as a most perfect and beautiful expression of her total dedication to God and as a model for women consecrated to God in this state. St Ambrose's tract on virginity would immediately come to mind in this context.[2]

Our second period is the eighth and ninth centuries. Theology was developing and had added a deeper sense of tradition to ongoing reflection on the Scriptures. New problems come from the newly evangelised tribes and from internal divisions in the empire. In the East there is the issue of images. It appeared to be a simple matter of whether the Old Testament prohibition of images (cf. Dt 4: 9-20) was still binding in the Christian dispensation. The deeper issue was, how are we to relate to the God who became visible in Christ Jesus? The fourth council of Constantinople (870) decided in favour of appropriate veneration of images of Christ, Mary, the angels and the saints.

In the West it was the age of Charlemagne which gave rise to a new vision of christendom ordered on earth through the emperor and towards heaven by its spiritual leaders. The idea of Mary as queen, though not absent in the earlier tradition, takes on a new prominence. One example from a poem ascribed in the Eastern Church to St John Damascene:

> I open my mouth and I will fill up in spirit,
> I pour forth speech to the Mother Queen;
> I look upon her with joyful praise;
> rejoicing I celebrate her miracles.[3]

At the same time her relationship to Christ is deeply pondered: she is seen to share already in the triumph of his resurrection and to have always been free from sin. More and more she is seen as the one who intercedes, and innumerable prayers are addressed to her. In this period, especially in the East there is exuberance in invocations. But, most significantly, the context in which we find praise of Mary is liturgical: sermons for her feasts, hymns for the offices and the Eucharistic liturgy.

Our third period is the golden age of scholasticism, the era of the great thirteenth century theologians, Albert the Great, Bonaventure and Thomas Aquinas. Their work was profoundly based on scripture, but they were perhaps the last of the great masters who were in full control of all areas of theology. The tradition of the Eastern fathers of the Church was re-discovered in the West at that time and put to best use by St Thomas. In addition, they were all concerned with a unification of the whole of theology. In their works, which were pre-dominantly christological, Mary has a clear role in the mystery of salvation. We find in the great medieval theologians not only a solid theology which places Mary in due relation to her son and as intercessor for humanity, but also deep piety in their sermons, hymns and prayers.

The thirteenth century was a century of quite extraordinary intellectual and cultural ferment. It was a high point of the feudal period in which each one had an assigned position and role to play. There was a total vision of the universe, of society, of mankind's destiny. Moreover, it was the period of rapid growth in secular literatures apart from Latin. It saw an enormous outcrop of popular legends about wars and chivalry. Courtly love would shortly be a pervasive ideology.

None of these features of medieval society was without influence on marian devotion and piety. Parallel to the secular legends which fed the imagination of European peoples, there arose in ever-increasing number legends about miraculous interventions and the power of Mary in the lives of individuals. In the great chain of being, Mary is seen in glory as the supreme intercessor. It is in this period that we find the great cathedrals being built with their soaring columns and arches leading the spirit upwards, together with a solemnity of liturgy which however, became increasingly remote for ordinary Christians. Popular piety would fill the void in people's lives. Medieval art would educate and inspire them.

Before we leave this period we might select for our illustration not one of the theological giants but a poet, Dante Alighieri, who wrote one of the supreme masterpieces of all literature, the *Divine Comedy*, in the first decades of the fourteenth century. The *Divine Comedy* is certainly the finest and perhaps the last expression of universal order. The poet who "midway in life's journey went astray to find himself alone in a dark wood" (*Inferno* 1: 1-3) is a symbol of mankind seeking the meaning of existence. He finds Mary concerned with him: the Virgin Mary takes pity on the poet, alone in the dark wood of error and she sends help to him (ibid 2: 94-96); it is her command that allows him to walk through the purification of purgatory (*Purgatorio* 1: 91-92), for in a sense she is the compassionate mother of purgatory; in the *Paradiso* hers is a beauty which is joy in the eyes of all the saints (*Paradiso* 31: 134-35).

In the Breviary we have the prayer which Bernard addresses to Mary in the translation of Ronald Knox. Perhaps a very literal translation, rather than the dense and more literary one in the *Liturgy of the Hours*, might capture best the spontaneity and spaciousness that Dante somehow achieves in his tight verse form:

> Virgin mother, daughter of your son,
> humble yet higher than any creature,
> the goal fixed by the eternal plan.

You are the one who so ennobled human nature
that its own Maker did not refuse
to be formed in it himself.

In your womb was set alight again
the love whose warmth in eternal peace
allowed that flower to blossom.

For those above you are the noonday torch,
while those below find in you
a living spring of hope.

O Lady so great and of such worth,
in seeking grace without recourse to you,
one would without wings attempt to fly.

In your kindness you look not only on those
who come to you, but you give help
to many even before they call.

In you is tenderness, in you is mercy,
in you is munificence; united in you
is all that is excellent in any creature.

(Paradiso 33: 1-21)[4]

The eminent mariologist Roschini stated the fundamental thesis of Dante to be: "no-one can come to God except through Christ, but no one can come to Christ except through Mary". Nonetheless, we may find already in Dante hints of what will lead to a serious decline in mariology.

Our fourth period is one of decline and stretches from the period of the great scholastics to the Counter-Reformation and beyond it to the age of the Enlightenment. One might look askance at the use of the word "decline". It seems to be a time of growth: there is a period of enormous literature on Mary, devotional as well as theological; shrines multiplied; art flourished; prayers, offices, hymns without number were composed; religious congregations devoted to Mary were founded; thousands of sermons by saints, theologians and clergy survive in manuscript and from earliest printed books. But it is the quality of this input that has to be questioned. Theology had become decadent: instead of being a quest for divine truth, theology became more and more an academic exercise, concerned more with words than with religious experience and holiness.

It was an age of darkness. Corruption in the Church was paralleled by pessimism in society. The Black Death of the fourteenth century gave rise to a darkness which pervaded the whole of society. Wars seemed never-ending. The idealism and optimism of the crusades had flickered out. The great vision of the whole world under a kindly providence encapsulated in the vision of the great chain of being underlying Dante's masterpiece became fragmented.

In this period, an image of Mary that had earlier roots comes much to the fore. From earliest times she was the intercessor. Now in the darkness of the later middle ages a dangerous development occurs. Christ becomes more and more a remote figure of divine justice and Mary is the figure of compassion, the hope of sinners. Many looked not to him as merciful saviour, but to his mother who is seen as the source of mercy. In extreme forms, this development is blasphemous and the reformers, as well as the saints and the better theologians, rightly protested. There is here some emphasis on the beauty of Mary, but it is divorced from sound theology. Legends and poetry depicting Mary as admitting to heaven those who would be rejected by Christ were certainly not absent. The underlying tendency to seek somehow through Mary what we might not get from Christ would persist in various guises right down to our century.

The reformers dealt a double blow to mariology, even though each of them did acknowledge some role for her in the divine plan. They rejected most of the popular devotions, not all of which were superstitious or distorted, though some undoubtedly were. On the other hand, their emphasis on scripture alone and their central concern to set aside all developments since the New Testament weakened mariology and isolated it. Later the period of Rationalism and the Enlightenment gave rise to pietism. Faced with an onslaught on traditional religion, many withdrew and, instead of seeking to counter the attacks of the critical and exaggerated supporters of reason, the Church in many instances retreated into a world of devotion and spirituality.

Hence one can claim that 1300-1800, though a time of

apparent growth in mariology, was in a sense a period of decline at a deeper level. The harmony needed between the three principles of Mary, as appropriately related to Christ, to us, and as a figure of beauty, was not on the whole well observed. Mariology became a separate branch of theology, becoming more and more divorced from the mainstream of the Church's theological reflection. It often tended to be over-apologetic or insufficiently critical. All this is not to suggest that the decline was total. But compared with earlier periods mariology was less healthy despite some theological treatises of distinction, many beautiful devotional writings and noble prayers and hymns. In a word, quantity is not necessarily the criterion of genuine growth.

Our final period is the mid-twentieth century. From the early 1900s there was great interest in the possibility of a definition of the Assumption following on the definition of the Immaculate Conception in 1854. There arose what is often called the marian movement which was particularly strong in the 1940s. Here again, there was an enormous volume of material concerned with the virgin. Interest centred on great celebrations of May and October as marian months, on Lourdes and Fatima, on the First Saturday. There was a phenomenal growth of pilgrimages, of Rosary crusades, of congresses, of devotional literature, as well as of marian organisations like the Legion of Mary, the Blue Army, in addition to new congregations of religious being founded in Europe and Africa which were dedicated to Mary as patron and model.

The Holy Year of 1950 marked a climax of the marian movement with the proclamation of the Assumption on 1 November. There followed the marian year of 1954, but even by then, perhaps, the marian movement was losing momentum.

Marian devotion received immense encouragement from papal statements, especially through Leo XIII at the end of the last century, Pius XI, and above all Pius XII who continued to write extensively on Mary until his death in 1958. These Roman pronouncements certainly fulfilled all the conditions necessary for a healthy mariology: they placed Mary in proper relationship with her son, with us, and they celebrated the beauty of the virgin. But the balance of papal encyclicals and sermons was not always retained by those who used them as a mine to extract statements about the mother of God for popular preaching.

Mariology continued to develop as a largely separate branch of theology with its own methodology and special concerns. With notable exceptions such as Newman, Scheeben, de la Taille, de Lubac, Congar and the Rahner brothers, the major theologians of these centuries did not give much attention to mariology. An unhealthy classification of mariology and mariologists appeared: works and their authors were categorised as maximalist and minimalist. These were theological approaches to the questions of marian theology and devotion. The maximalist approach tended to give more weight to traditional interpretations of scripture, to apparitions, to new feasts and devotions and to the possibility of a new defintion of Mary as mediatrix. The minimalists, so called, were on the whole more interested in what was already established in theology, in liturgy and in devotion than with innovation.

A turning point in mariology was the first Mariological-Marian Congress in Lourdes (1958). It broke away from the theologically unsound and highly emotive division of maximalism and minimalism to see marian theology as having a double focus: christological and ecclesiological. In the first, the mysteries of Mary, viz. the Immaculate Conception, divine motherhood, perpetual virginity and Assumption, are related to her role in the mystery of Christ. In the second approach these same mysteries are seen in relation to the Church. One could illustrate these two by showing them paralleled in the prefaces of the Assumption and Immaculate Conception in the revised missal, e.g. the preface for the Immaculate Conception:

> Father, all powerful and ever-living God,
> we do well always and everywhere to give you thanks.
> (*christological*) You allowed no stain of Adam's sin
>   to touch the Virgin Mary.
> Full of grace, she was to be a worthy mother of your Son,
> (*ecclesiological*) your sign of favour to the Church
>   at its beginning,
> and the promise of its perfection as the bride of Christ,
>   radiant in beauty.
> (*christological*) Purest of virgins, she was to bring forth
>   your Son,
> the innocent lamb who takes away our sins.

(*ecclesiological*) You chose her from all women
to be our advocate with you and our pattern of holiness.

The Second Vatican Council (1962-1965) was the first council to speak directly on Mary — all previous ones which made marian statements were primarily concerned with other aspects of doctrine. She is mentioned in twelve of the sixteen documents of the Council. A serious conflict arose in the Council about its main statement on Mary. Some bishops wanted a separate document on her, but in the end, by the narrowest vote in the entire four years, it was decided (1114 to 1074) that the Council's major utterance on Mary would be a chapter of the Constitution on the Church. As it finally appeared the document would reflect a christological approach and an ecclesiological one set side by side (nn. 51-59 and 60-69 respectively). At the end of the third session (1964), during which the Constitution on the Church had been promulgated, Pope Paul VI proclaimed Mary as Mother of the Church. This at first sight would seem to favour the ecclesiological approach to mariology, but the text of the Pope's address is, however, markedly christological. One might mention as an aside that devotional forms that are prescribed by popes often do not take root in the religious sensibility of the Church: one might instance the feast of Our Lady Queen of Heaven (Pius XIII), Joseph the Worker (Pius XII), the solemn status given to the feast of the Precious Blood (John XXIII) and the title Mother of the Church (Paul VI). Devotions normally arise from the grass roots of religious experience.

After the Council there was a period of decline in devotion to Mary. The causes for this are complex. Some factors could be instanced. Popularisation of the findings of strict biblical exegesis led to insecurity in preachers who felt that their former use of the scriptures might not be legitimate. The refusal of the Second Vatican Council to produce an independent document on Mary or to develop new marian doctrines was sometimes misinterpreted as downplaying Mary. More importantly, the Church's main energies were concentrated on liturgical reform, on institutional renewal and on ecumenism. Marian devotion was not the only casualty in the decade following the Council: there was serious decline in the whole area of non-liturgical piety, not least due to the proliferation of Masses in places and circumstances where hitherto there had been other prayer forms such as novenas, sodalities and confraternities, usually with Benediction of the Blessed Sacrament. Attempts to retain devotions, or even Benediction, as part of, or an appendage to Mass were rightly frowned upon by liturgists. But in the end devotions had, as it were, nowhere to go. Again, ecumenism had been seriously adopted by the Church only with the establishment of the Secretariat for Christian Unity by John XXIII (1960) and the Decree on Ecumenism of Vatican II (1964). In what was for the Catholic Church the early days of ecumenism, there was, understandably, an emphasis on what could be shared by other Christians rather than what was divisive between them. Other major issues of the late 1960s and early 1970s were social questions, a growing alienation from the institutions of the Church, a decline in explicit faith, increasing secularism and general confusion in the minds of people and their priests, particularly on moral issues. None of this augured well for devotional life. Compared with other periods of decline, which were more of a distortion of the role of Mary, the decade from 1965-75 was characterised by apathy and neglect of Mary in many areas of Church life.

The apostolic exhortation of Paul VI, *Marialis cultus* (*To Honour Mary*, CTS, 1974) was to be a second turning point for mariology in our life-time. As this congress will in several ways show, the future for mariology will lie in its being, as Pope Paul demanded, liturgical, biblical, ecumenical and anthropological. Marian devotion will be expressed in liturgy, have its roots in the scriptures, be enriched and corrected by ecumenical sensitivity and take full account of Mary as woman and thus model for men and women of today. It would, I think, be fair to say that the riches and orientation of this magnificent document have yet to be deeply explored and appropriated by the Church as a whole.

I would end by referring briefly to one of the most original and creative theologians to have emerged in the Church since perhaps, the middle ages, Hans Urs von Balthasar. Karl Rahner once described his achievements as "breath-taking", but his major works are only now beginning to appear in English. He constantly refers to Mary in his theological writing. But it is in his overall perspective of theology that we find profoundly exemplified, the triple axis of Mary related to Christ, to the Church and as the beautiful one. One of von

Balthasar's enduring triumphs is the rediscovery of beauty as the form, the key, in fact, to the mystery of God's relationship to humanity in Christ Jesus. Beauty for von Balthasar is not an accidental quality added to salvation history: it is the only way that we can really see it properly. And the supreme moment of beauty and glory is Calvary where in the utter poverty of God there is infinite richness in love.

Again and again, von Balthasar returns to the Annunciation story in St Luke. Here he finds the origin of the Church, its deepest meaning. For in Mary's virginal consent there is the never-ending programme for the Church, for it opens the Church to the infinite possibilities of God's self-bestowing love. The only full expression of its reality is a catholicity that is found in the doctrine of the Communion of Saints in which all of humanity, to the extent that its members are in Christ, are the beneficiaries of Mary's "yes" at the Annunciation and reflect it. As such they enjoy her intercession and maternal care. Being marian is not an option for the Church; it is the only way in which it is truly open to Christ. The Church must share with Mary the beauty of the God-forsakenness of the cross so that in total emptiness it may find through obedience the way of love, love above all that is received before it is returned.

In this vision of von Balthasar,[5] which many lectures could not adequately unfold, there are seeds for a new development in mariology, one which fully accords with the norms of Pope Paul VI and, moreover, shows a way forward to further growth. Mariology is invited to grow not by further studies or new devotional forms but through ceaseless contemplation of the virgin who in the very heart of the Church, leads the Church to an understanding of the core of its own being. At this level we need not worry about the distortions of mariology, for all finds a unity.

Mary is the beautiful one who gave Christ his body, so that he, the New Adam, in turn might, from this same body, find a fit companion for himself in the Church, the New Eve born from his side on the cross. (cf. Gen 2: 20-24; Jn 19: 25-28 the Woman; Eph 5: 23-27; these texts with Lk 1: 26-38 are central to von Balthasar's mariology). And the Church was in Mary even before it was institutionalised in Peter. She was already a fit companion for him, "without spot or wrinkle. . . holy and without blemish" in her virginal consent. The vision of Mary and the Church, becomes blurred, the more deeply we enter into the mystery of the virginal mother and the bridal mother. The mother of the spouse is herself the summit of the bride's response. It is then in a deepened theology of the Church as bride, as mother, as body, as the Communion of Saints that there is a way for profound growth for mariology, perhaps in von Balthasar's direction, but at any rate not neglecting the rich insights he has rediscovered for us often in the Fathers of the Church.

3

THE IMMACULATE CONCEPTION AND ASSUMPTION OF OUR LADY IN TODAY'S THINKING

Michael O'Carroll, CSSp

Before thinking of problems arising out of the two dogmas proclaimed by the Popes in 1854 and 1950 it may be well to ensure a clear understanding of what each means, and to recall, if only briefly, the pre-history in each case. We must treat them separately to get through this necessary doctrinal and historical background.

Immaculate Conception

First, then, the Immaculate Conception. In the Apostolic Constitution, *Ineffabilis Deus,* on 8 December 1854, Pius IX solemnly defined the truth in these words:

> Accordingly, by the inspiration of the Holy Spirit, for the honour of the holy and undivided Trinity, for the glory and adornment of the Virgin Mother of God, for the exaltation of the Catholic faith, and for the furtherance of the Catholic religion, by the authority of Jesus Christ our Lord, of the Blessed Apostles Peter and Paul, and by our own: We declare, pronounce, and define that the doctrine which holds that the most Blessed Virgin Mary, in the first instant of her conception, by a singular grace and privilege granted by Almighty God, in view of the merits of Jesus Christ, the Saviour of the human race, was preserved free from all stain of original sin, is a doctrine revealed by God and therefore to be believed firmly and constantly by all the faithful.

This pronouncement was the climax, the happy, irreversible conclusion to a long, acrimonious, at times tormented debate. Nowhere in Sacred Scripture do we read, in explicit terms, that Mary was conceived immaculate. The texts used to show that it is *implied* are: Genesis 3:15 — "I will put enmity between you and the woman"; Luke 1:28 — "Full of grace", words which would be better replaced for accuracy by "Highly-favoured one"; Luke 1:42 —"Blessed art thou among women".

Pius IX, in the lengthy introduction to the dogmatic definition, drew on Sacred Scripture in combination with the Fathers of the Church.

When did the idea emerge in Tradition? Cardinal Newman did write that he drew the doctrine from the patristic teaching on Mary as the New Eve found in St Irenaeus, St Justin Martyr and Tertullian from the second century; but few would go beyond saying that there is implicit harmony between the two ideas. If Mary was truly the New Eve she must be at least equal to the first Eve in original innocence.

The first apparently explicit testimony is in the Nisibene hymns of St Ephraem, a fourth century Syrian writer: "Certainly you alone and your mother are from every aspect completely beautiful, for there is no blemish in you, my Lord, and no stain in your mother." But there are other texts in the same author's writings which, to put it mildly, call for subtle interpretation to maintain this doctrine — he spoke for example of Mary's baptism.

The opinion of St Ambrose is also controverted; he did first establish the complete personal sinlessness of Mary. St Augustine held this latter doctrine; his opinion on the Immaculate Conception is endlessly debated. His much-quoted text "except the holy Virgin Mary, about whom, for the honour of the Lord, I want there to be no question" is offset by some enigmatic words which he used to counter the taunt of Julian of Eclanum, a Pelagian who said to him "you deliver Mary herself to the devil through the condition of her birth." Unfortunately, in another way, Augustine's negative influence on the development of the doctrine was for centuries decisive. He thought that original sin was transmitted by conjugal intercourse through inherent concupiscence. Christ was immune because he was conceived virginally — the conclusion was drawn that Mary was not.

I shall not quote further texts which encourage a view that the doctrine was being clearly grasped in the East and the West. Some of these texts while emphatic on the immunity from original sin, do not always specify the precise moment.

One must admit that, as well as Ambrose and Augustine, the

great Latin Doctors took an opposing view. St Anselm denied the doctrine, though it could find a place within his general description of Mary's holiness, "a degree of purity than which no greater can be imagined apart from God." He also taught that original sin was an absence of original justice, which would minimise the factor of concupiscence in transmission. St Bernard, a mighty name in the history of marian piety and spirituality, denied the doctrine; but he would submit to the decision of Rome. St Albert the Great was satisfied with sanctification in the womb; St Bonaventure shared this view but he did admit that God could have given Mary the privilege. St Thomas Aquinas also held the doctrine of sanctification in the womb. He rendered a service to development of doctrine by his insistence on the universality of redemption by Christ, which must include Mary. In this he was joined by Alexander of Hales. These and others did not see how Mary could be conceived immaculate and yet be held, as she must, to owe all her grace to Christ.

This is a formidable body of learned opinion. How did the doctrine succeed in obtaining any recognition, in persisting? The liturgy played a notable part. The history of the feast in the west, for instance its early appearance in Ireland, is uncertain. It existed in England, possibly brought by some eastern monk towards 1060, disappeared after the Norman conquest, in 1066, was revived about 1127/8, and passed thereafter into Normandy, France, Belgium, Spain and Germany. The importance of the feast in the development of the doctrine was immense. It ensured a foundation which is always indispensable to doctrine, the *sensus fidei*, the conviction of the faithful. Theologians sought to explain what precisely was the object of the feast.

Other factors counted. Theologians, chiefly in England, defended the doctrine, Eadmer, OSB, for instance, secretary and biographer of St Anselm and then the giant Duns Scotus, who broke out of the impasse described by St Thomas: he taught that Mary could have been redeemed by *preservation*, by anticipation if you wish, as all others are by *liberation*. This privilege came from the perfect Mediator. In 1439, a council held in Basle declared for the doctrine. It did not have the authority of a general Church council for it had broken with the Pope.

The Popes themselves chose to intervene in a debate which flared up violently at times: the opposing ranks were Franciscans and Dominicans, the latter against the doctrine out of loyalty to St Thomas, the former defending it in the tradition of Duns Scotus. But the Dominicans had the whip hand through control of the Holy Office, the Roman Inquisition. Sixtus IV, a Franciscan Pope, issued two Apostolic Constitutions on the matter: he forbade one side to call those on the other heretics, and he approved a Mass of the Immaculate Conception to be said in Rome. At a time when universities counted mightily in the formation of opinion, many of the European universities followed the example of Paris which in 1497 decreed that henceforth those admitted to degrees must take an oath to defend the Immaculate Conception. Then the Council of Trent, in 1546, by its assertion exempting Mary from its decree on original sin gave a subtle pointer to the ultimate positive formulation:

> This holy Synod declares, nevertheless, that it is not its intention to include in this decree, where original sin is treated of, the blessed and immaculate Virgin Mary, Mother of God, but that the constitutions of Pope Sixtus IV of happy memory are to be observed, under the penalties contained in these constitutions which it renews.

Further papal interventions followed, all moving in the direction of approval of the doctrine. Controversy blazed in the seventeenth century, a golden age of marian theology, spirituality and oratory. This was the time when kings vowed their realms to Our Lady. So the kings of Spain exerted pressure on the papacy to proclaim the doctrine — one of the delegations was led by the brilliant Irish Franciscan, Luke Wadding.

The new religious institutes were now active in the debate, or should I say spate; between 1600 and 1800 the Jesuits alone brought out 300 works on the Immaculate Conception. Hippolyto Marracci, of the Clerks Regular of the Mother of God, the most prolific author in history on Our Lady, — he composed 115 books on her — was an ardent champion of the Immaculate Conception (a friend of Luke Wadding, incidentally). Using a pseudonym he infringed a rule made by the Inquisition and used the words "Immaculate Conception" in the titles of two books. He was discovered and put under some sort of house arrest. His biographer says that he never wrote better.

If that was one extreme, there was another: this was the vow taken by some to defend the "pious opinion" as the doctrine was called, even to the shedding of their blood. This practice was sharply criticised by Muratori, the father of Italian history.

On 8 December 1667, a landmark was reached. Pope Alexander VII issued the bull *Sollicitudo omnium Ecclesiarum* in reply to the request of Philip IV of Spain. Without condemning the opposing opinion, the Pope manifested the preference of the Holy See for the doctrine and protected it. Pius IX's definition in *Ineffabilis Deus* brought some amendments to this formulation, and added the obligation of assent by believing Catholics; but the parallel, at 200 years distance, is noteworthy; the opposition declined thereafter.

The liturgy and popular devotion were to help achieve peace after the passion of debate. On 15 May 1695, Innocent XII imposed on the whole Church the Office and Mass of the Immaculate Conception, with Octave; on 6 December 1708, Clement XI established the feast as a holyday of obligation. Marian theology and devotion went into general decline during the eighteenth and early nineteenth centuries and this affected speculation, or lack of it, on the Immaculate Conception. The revival came from the unexpected source, the Miraculous Medal in 1830. This emblem was distributed to millions. The prayer was: "O Mary, conceived without sin, pray for us who have recourse to thee."

This prayer undoubtedly prepared the faithful for the dogma, but it was not the motivating force of Pius IX. He first made a consultation of the entire hierarchy of the Church (*Ubi primum*, 2 February 1849)[1] and found it practically unanimous on the subject. Then he set cardinals and theologians to work on the composition of an appropriate text. Two theologians prominent in Rome, Carlo Passaglia and Giovanni Perrone, SJ, had specialised in the doctrine of the Immaculate Conception. Newman, then in Rome, was impressed by the work of Perrone, as he was by the Pope's desire to know the sentiment of the faithful. A French Benedictine, better known as a liturgist, Dom Gueranger, made a valuable contribution.

Altogether eight drafts of the text were prepared. The cardinals in consistory approved the second last schema; then the Pope consulted four cardinals, among them the Englishman Wiseman, who had sent him suggestions.

It was not an age of critical scholarship and the mode of composition saved the introductory matter which led up to the defining formula from the effects of this deficiency: the Pope decided to present the teaching of the Fathers and the belief of the Church in globo. There were practically no footnotes, few references to Fathers. The historical review gives importance to Alexander VII, who in the lengthy passage cited names other Popes.

For completeness I add that St Pius X in the encyclical *Ad diem illum* and Pius XII in the encyclical *Fulgens corona* recalled the dogma, and the essential words "preserved free from all stain of original sin" were written into the Constitution on the Church, published by Vatican II (*LG* 59).

Assumption

Thus far we have considered the dogma on the first moment of Mary's earthly existence. We turn to the second dogma which deals with the last moments of her life on earth. It will take less time if I may reassure you. On 1 November 1950 Pius XII published the Apostolic Constitution *Munificentissimus Deus.* The essential words of the dogma were:

> We pronounce, declare and define it to be ever Virgin Mary having completed the course of her earthly life, was assumed body and soul to heavenly glory.

Once again we must admit that there is no explicit biblical witness to this mystery. When we come to examine tradition we have to deal with two distinct types of testimony. There are first the Assumption Apocrypha — first in time, not intrinsic importance — the different versions of a basic legend coming down from ancient times on Mary's death and assumption into heaven. Until recently these stories, *transitus* as they are called, were not accorded very much status in early Christian literature. They are more highly valued now for two reasons: there have been a number of documentary finds, that is hitherto unknown versions, and the dating has been pushed back to very near the actual event, possibly as early as the second century. The versions recently discovered are an early Greek *Transitus* and simultaneously a Latin translation of it, a Georgian *Transitus* and especially one in Ethiopian which seems very near to the original text.

I note in passing that the Ethiopian version is remarkably like the one hitherto taken as nearest to the primeval, the Syriac. It is of interest to us to observe the similarity of the early Irish version with both the Syriac and and the Ethiopian. It is continental scholars, Victor Arras of Louvain and Michel van Esbroeck of Brussels who have drawn attention to the importance of this early Irish document. Arras, in particular, regrets that more attention has not been given to it and deplores the fact that it is so difficult to obtain; the last edition was in 1942 by an American scholar. The basic scenario in all the Assumption Apocrypha is the miraculous arrival of the Apostles at Mary's deathbed, the coming of the Lord and of the angels, especially St Michael, the rising of first Mary's soul, and then her body to heaven, where they are united. Not all versions relate the union, i.e. the complete bodily glorification. Interestingly the very early ones do — the other idea is a kind of separate existence of soul and body beyond the grave.

Pius XII did not mention these Apocrypha in the historical review which in the Apostolic Constitution, *Munificentissimus Deus*, precedes the dogmatic formula I have quoted. He does quote some of the Fathers of the Church, St John of Damascus (d.c. 749-753), an early sermon, attributed to Modestus of Jerusalem, a seventh century writer, others notably St Germanus of Constantinople. Since the year in which he defined the dogma a very important testimony, a hitherto unknown homily on the Assumption by Theoteknos of Livias, dating from the sixth century, was discovered by a great Byzantine scholar, Fr Antoine Wenger, AA.

By the eighth century the doctrine was firmly and fully accepted in the East. Development was slower in the West, for a strange reason. Apart from doubt expressed by Adamnan, who influenced Bede, two bogus texts halted acceptance of the truth: one a pseudo-Augustinian sermon and the other a pseudo-Jerome letter. The author of the first was the eighth century Ambrose Autpert, and of the second, the ninth century Paschasius Radbert. In medieval times certain names carried immense authority, St Jerome certainly, still more so St

Augustine. Why then the obvious thing, in reply to such fabrications was to put into circulation another treatise for the Assumption and give it the name of Augustine: so pseudo-Augustine gradually eclipsed pseudo-Jerome. In addition Eastern Greek homilies defending the Assumption were available as was a patchwork piece of oratory made up from all of them. The result of this and of liturgical practice was that from the thirteenth century every important western writer held the doctrine: Pius XII quotes from a select number.

Why did he define as a dogma a truth which by our time had become an accepted part of our belief? Did he use the Assumption to sidetrack a bigger problem, the possible definition of Mary's universal mediation? He told Cardinal Tardini a few days after his election that he would define the dogma.

He did not rush into it. He adopted the same procedure as Pius IX in regard to the Immaculate Conception. Though conscious of a very widespread demand he consulted the entire hierarchy of the Church and got a very favourable response.[2] He set up a drafting committee to secure a good text: the names of the members are known to us, two of them eminent for scholarly works on the Assumption, the French Augustinian, Fr Martin Jugie, and the Croatian Franciscan, Fr Karl Balic. In the course of the deliberations of this group two things emerged. One committee member, Fr Lennerz, a professor at the Gregorian University in Rome, did not think that the doctrine could be defined as a dogma, as he thought it necessary to show a clear historical tradition going back to the event of the Assumption and, at the time, he knew that this was impossible. When the Pope pronounced the definition he made an act of faith. It is interesting to note that the historical link does not seem beyond the bounds of research now. An archaeological expert in the Holy Land, Fr Bellarmino Bagatti, OFM, for a while thought that he might show a connection between the legend and the results of his research into Our Lady's grave which he has located in Gethsemane.

The second point brought to the Pope's notice by Fr Jugie was the impossibility of declaring infallibly that Our Lady died. Pius XII accepted this advice and used a non-committal formula in regard to the end of Mary's life "when the course of her earthly life was completed". Immediately a debate began

on the problem. The same phrase is used in the brief reference
to the Assumption by Vatican II (*LG* 59). Note also that there
was no agreement in the committee on the scriptural, i.e.
implicit scriptural, warrant for the dogma. The Pope appealed
to the close union between Mary and Christ and to their
identity in the victory over sin and death. Though he spoke of
Sacred Scripture as the ultimate basis, he really based his
definition on the faith of the Church.

The dogmas today
But it is time to come to grips with the problems which the two
dogmas may raise at the present time. Here the issue is mostly
ecumenical. From the separated brethren of the western
Churches the objection is generally that there is an absence of
biblical warrant. An example to illustrate the position is in the
*Final Report of the Anglican/Roman Catholic International
Commission;* this body was set up by Paul VI and Archbishop
Ramsey in 1966 and its first report on the Eucharist was little
short of sensational.

It is the subsequent report on Authority that concerns us
here. The principal subject considered under the last heading
was the papacy, and infallibility was discussed at length. The
Commission, in this context, expressed an opinion on marian
questions relevant to the subject of our paper. Paragraph 29
deals with the conditions needed for a binding decision issued
by the Bishop of Rome and ends thus:

> When it is plain that all these conditions have been
> fulfilled, Roman Catholics conclude that the judgement
> is preserved from error and the proposition true. If the
> definition proposed for assent were not manifestly a
> legitimate interpretation of biblical faith and in line with
> orthodox tradition Anglicans would think it a duty to
> reserve the reception of the definition for study and
> discussion.

Paragraph 30 applies this general idea to the marian doctrine
and dogmas of the Catholic Church:

> This approach is illustrated by the reaction of many
> Anglicans to the Marian definitions, which are the only
> examples of such dogmas promulgated by the Bishop of
> Rome apart from a synod (i.e. a general Church council)

since the separation of our two communions. . .

There follow a series of expressions of agreement between Roman Catholics and Anglicans — Mary's position subordinate to that of Christ, her relationship to Christ and the Church, her unique grace and vocation as *Theotokos*, on the celebration of her festivals, that she is a model of holiness, faith and obedience, a prophetic figure of God before as after the Incarnation.

> Nevertheless, the dogmas of the Immaculate Conception and the Assumption raise a special problem for those Anglicans who do not consider that the precise definitions given by these dogmas are sufficiently supported by Scripture. For many Anglicans the teaching authority of the Bishop of Rome, independent of a Council, is not recommended by the fact that through it these Marian doctrines were proclaimed as dogmas binding on all the faithful. Anglicans would also ask whether, in any future union between our Churches, they would be required to subscribe to such dogmatic statements. One consequence of our separation has been a tendency for Anglicans and Roman Catholics alike to exaggerate the importance of the Marian dogmas in themselves at the expense of other truths more closely related to the foundation of the Christian faith.

When Dr Donald Coogan, Dr Ramsey's successor as Archbishop of Canterbury, visited Pope Paul VI in Rome in April 1977 he was quite frank on the subject of the marian dogmas; he described them as "still presenting great difficulties for Anglicans." I should say that the Final Report has an important note which reads as follows:

> The affirmation of the Roman Catholic Church that Mary was conceived without original sin is based on recognition of her unique role within the mystery of the Incarnation. By being thus prepared to be the mother of our Redeemer she also becomes a sign that the salvation by Christ was operative among all mankind before his birth. The affirmation that her glory in heaven involves full participation in the fruits of salvation expresses and reinforces our faith that the life of the world to come has already broken into the life of our world. It is the conviction of Roman Catholics that the Marian dogmas formulate a faith consonant with Scripture.

Nearer home a working party was set up by the Bally-mascanlon Conference to consider "Church, Scripture and Authority"[3]. The findings and opinions set down in their report, presented in 1981, complement the views emanating from the Anglicans, which are also echoed in various documents issued by the Church of Scotland. Each Christian communion expounded its marian doctrine or tradition. The Roman Catholics were at pains to show how the formulation of dogma may with time be perfected, without any change in the inner meaning. They also made it clear that they do not support isolation of marian teaching and devotion, and are vigilant against excesses. The Immaculate Conception is shown as an expression of the "totality of the work of grace in the order of redemption", "the signal act of God's prevenient grace", entirely appropriate "in view of Mary's unique relationship to her divine son". The Assumption is explained as articulating "certain truths integral to the gospel". It is as a "paradigm of our redemption", and "exemplar of the Church" that Mary is the embodiment of "God's grace realised in human holiness".

These are examples of the thinking noted among the separated brethren of the West, chosen, so to speak, near home to give them added point and immediate relevance. In the East, among the Orthodox the main objection would not be biblical. For the Easterns are not so rigidly attached to literal interpretation of Sacred Scripture — for them tradition coming from the apostolic age may imply scripture if it does not englobe it. Opposition to the doctrine of the Immaculate Conception has not been official among the Orthodox until recent centuries. Some of the greatest Orthodox writers, St Gregory Palamas in the fourteenth century and the expatriate Russian Sergius Bulgakov in the present century (d. 1944), though not defending the Immaculate Conception, so phrase their language on Mary's sinlessness that it almost amounts to our view. When Easterns do object it is very often through fear that Mary may be removed from the human condition. In regard to the Assumption the Orthodox have no difficulty, but they insist that Our Lady died and object to the non-committal formula used by Pius XII.

Here we come to the nub of the question. These are papal dogmas, in the essential moment the teaching not of a general council, but of a Pope; and though the Pope, in each case, consulted the bishops, the separated brethren did not benefit by this consultation. Each Pope imposed on Catholics the duty of believing. To refuse belief, said Pius XII was to fall away from the "divine and Catholic faith". Pius IX used an equivalent phrase.

How do we carry this papal load in the climate of the ecumenical age? First I think that we have to make it clear that each dogma was not an arbitrary, sudden innovation, a highly personal act of the Pope. Each came at the end of a long process of development, was, within the body of the faithful, in the final moment, seen to be above and free of debate. Nor did the Pope act in splendid isolation: he called in the best theological experts available. More importantly, as we have seen, he consulted the bishops in communion with the Holy See. Those who object to a dogma defined without the consent of all Christian Churches would in effect deprive us of the magisterium until complete Christian unity is achieved. Even at Vatican II the separated brethren were present only as observers.

No responsible Catholic theologian that I know of has challenged the competence of the Pope in the matter. Nor have any objected that, in the case of the Assumption, the Pope should not have done what Vatican I refused to do. In 1870 the suggestion had been made that the Assumption be defined by the Council. Though supported by some 200 bishops the proposal was turned down.

Time does not allow me to deal with the theology of original sin — on which East and West tend to diverge anyway — or of the Resurrection as the prototype of the Assumption. Let me say that neither dogma is adversely affected by any genuine advance in theological research or reflection.

I would not like either to embark here on a discussion of the doctrine of Vatican II on the "hierarchy of truths" and its possible application to marian doctrine as a whole or in its particulars. To give all the nuances or shades of opinion needed would take too much space. It has been well said that this idea of the hierarchy of truths is a beautiful concept until you try to work it out in practical detail. I personally fail to see how two dogmas which have engaged the greatest intellects in the history of Christendom, which have been elaborated after

55

centuries of hard thinking can be relegated to some inferior position in our theological system. I say all this speaking as a worker in the cause of Christian Unity since the very first years of my priesthood over forty years ago, in the Mercier Society (of which I was a founder member) in which with others I suffered for this noble cause — from my fellow-Catholics at different levels — a cause which I intend to serve until the end of my days.

If I am asked whether I believe that these dogmas will prove an obstacle to the ecumenical movement I answer "No". I believe in miracles. I saw something of a miracle in Blackrock College at the international congress of the Ecumenical Society of the Blessed Virgin Mary, when an American Presbyterian, Donald Dawe, faced in a brilliant lecture the problem of the Immaculate Conception, as his friend and co-religionist, Ross Mackenzie, has shown that he is prepared to do for the other dogma. I recall a piquant remark made by the Methodist Gordon Wakefield, in his message to the ecumenical congress: Mary must help us to unite. She is no longer considered an obstacle. Archbishop Runcie also expressed the hope that the congress would show that Mary cannot be a subject of division among the followers of her son.

So the Lady stands before history and within divine revelation of which she is part and an instrument, in the splendour of her initial innocence and in her culminating personal glory, body and soul, our "life, our sweetness and our hope".[4]

4

MARY IN ECUMENICAL DIALOGUE[1]

Alberic Stacpoole, OSB

Any such study as this runs up against the problem of how to go about it. Are we to march chronologically down the years of Church history? Are we to move from one denomination to another, painting a spectrum of traditions? Are we to hop from one subject to another within the possible theological panorama? Are we to take the data of scripture in some ordered fashion? Or are we to weave all of these together in some coherent tapestry? It seems that the last is the *via media*, but that time is the clearest measure and a good control approach: "as the centuries go by, the Church is always advancing towards the plenitude of her divine truth, until eventually the words of God are fulfilled in her."[2] Christ projects himself to us in time and space, history being his servant; and so also does his mother manifest herself as age follows age, so that each generation "will call me blessed", and in so doing reveal the *Theotokos* or God-bearer and indeed God himself.

Mary is part of revelation; not just evidence-revealed, but person-revealing, throwing light on the process of God's revelation itself. The Eve-Mary typology, brought to consciousness very early in the Church's life, indeed by the second century Fathers (notably St Irenaeus) illustrates God's preferred means of enlightening us, not with inordinate haste, but progressively and in due time, yielding to the contemplative as much as to the analyst: context, previous history and future unfolding all play their part. As biblical theologians and Council Fathers have long insisted, there is a wholeness in revelation, and especially a unity in the corpus of scripture. All revelation is proximate to the mystery of Christ; and, as the Council Fathers at Vatican II have stated, none is more indissolubly linked than that of mother and Redeemer-son. From this it has been argued that the nearer a person is to

Christ in life, vocation, grace, the more fully is that person the bearer of revelation: whoever is able to open to us the inexhaustible treasure of Christ thereby discloses the divine mind. By that token, Mary is then the handmaid of revelation into the deepest mystery of divinity.[3]

Mary in ecumenism before the Council
Massive ecumenical initiatives were liberated by the Vatican Council and the work of the Secretariat for Promoting Christian Unity (SPCU) in the 1960s, so that the Catholic Church is now involved in depth in a dozen international dialogues and even more at regional and national levels. Because the Anglican Communion has its "special place" so near to the Catholic,[4] and because its moral centre is Canterbury/Lambeth (the Archbishop of Canterbury being, in a loose and unconstitutional sense, president of the Anglican Communion and Chairman of the Lambeth Conference each decade); and because of the predominance of the English speaking world in all the activities of the free world, one tends to see ecumenism in the field as most intensely expressed in our time in the British Isles. In the 1950s, it was France and Germany that led the thought of the Church as it bubbled up into the Conciliar years;[5] but since then it would be fair to say that the initiative has moved to the British spheres (including Australasia and South Africa) and to North America (Canada playing its own distinctive part).[6]

In that light, it is worth our recalling how much these islands have been dedicated down the last millennium to both study of and devotion to the Blessed Virgin Mary.[7] From the days of Bede in Northumbria, the monks, canons and friars — dedicating their abbeys and second altars to *Sancta Maria* —have included her in their writings and their liturgies. Eadmer and Anselm of Canterbury, Osbert de Clare of Westminster, Aelred of Rievaulx, Nicholas of St Albans and the several Williams, of Malmesbury, Newburgh, Nottingham and Ware were all worthy precursors of the great Duns Scotus of Oxford. Arguably the doctrine of the Immaculate Conception arose from such communities keeping and reflecting upon the feast of the Conception of the Virgin: piety and theology progress together, the need calling forth the reasoning (as *fides quaerens intellectum*).[8] So much was this so that the last of the Archbishops of Canterbury to visit Rome until modern times, Thomas Arundel (in 1397), recorded that in the universal Church the title "Dowry of Mary" was accorded to the English.

Enthusiasm did indeed lead to abuse, piety degenerating into superstition; but official teaching held true even into the Reformation period.[9] The *Ten Articles* of 1536, the first Anglican confession of faith, enjoined respect for "the four holy Councils", which included Ephesus at which the title *Theotokos* was canonised. Images were approved as "kindlers and stirrers of men's minds", especially images of Christ and his mother; though there were warnings made against "censing, kneeling or offering to them". Intercession of the saints was encouraged to obtain grace: "We may pray to our Blessed Lady, to St John the Baptist, to all and every of the apostles and to any other saint particularly as our devotion doth serve us." The Bishops' Book of 1537 and the King's Book of 1543 are both, concerning Mary, unexceptionable. It was the *Thirty Nine Articles*, finally issued in 1571, after the brief interlude of the Catholic monarch, Mary, followed by Elizabeth's courting of Catholicism, which moved England to Protestantism in marian matters as well.

Article VI that "Holy Scripture containeth all things necessary to salvation", was taken to foreclose any sense of traditional development, especially in doctrine, and more especially marian dogma. Article XV, that "if we say we have no sin, we deceive ourselves", implied (for those who wished it) a denial of the Immaculate Conception. Article XXII, that "the Romish doctrine concerning Purgatory, Pardons, Worshipping and Adoration, as well of Images as of Reliques, and also the invocation of Saints, is a fond thing vainly invented, and grounded upon no warranty of Scripture, but rather repugnant to the Word of God", comprehensively assailed marian piety. Thus the Walsingham shrine was destroyed with other shrines, marian statues were broken up, holy places were obliterated, liturgical veneration of Mary was removed from the Prayer Book, invocations were forbidden — but doctrine was not re-written, though silenced until it might pertain again.

Once the noise of denominational battle was stilled and a more reflective period was ushered in, once the Anglican Church had become sufficiently settled to allow of confident reflection, the seventeenth century interpreters of the faith often displayed a wistfulness toward the old marian devotion. Nowhere was this given more classic expression than in the little poem of George Herbert, the divine (1593-1633), *To all angels and saints*:

> . . . I would address
> My vows to thee most gladly, Blessed Maid,
> And mother of my God, in my distress.
> Thou art the holy mine, whence came the gold,
> The great restorative for all decay
> In young and old;
> Thou art the cabinet whence the jewel lay:
> Chiefly to thee would I my soul unfold:
> But now, alas, I dare not; for our King,
> Whom we do all joyntly adore and praise,
> Bids no such thing. . .

This submerged theme in Anglican devotion persisted down the years even into our own time: we find it, for instance, in the work of a Great War poet, where — in *Good Friday falls on Lady Day* — he has this to say:

> And has Our Lady lost her place,
> Does her white star burn dim?
> Nay, she has lowly veiled her face
> Because of him.
> Men give to her the jeweled crown
> And robe with broidered rim,
> But she is fain to cast them down
> Because of him.
> She claims no crown from Christ apart,
> Who gave God life and limb;
> She only claims a broken heart
> Because of him.[10]

This theme, this weakness of doctrine and reluctance to pursue conviction, can be found even at the heart of the most respected of Anglican theologians. A divine as perceptive as John Keble seemed unnerved when he came to mariology. Though he published his *Lyra innocentium* (Oxford, 1846), replete with references to Mary, as the Tractarian Movement was breaking down, he had not the courage to include even this exceedingly ambivalent poem, appropriately entitled

Mary out of sight (written in 1844), among that collection of children's meditations: his friends' persuasions prevailed, and the poem remained out of sight until publication of Keble's *Miscellaneous Poems* (Oxford, 1870) four years after his death. A poem of weakness, it weakly prospered: of that, the reader is left to judge —

> Mother of God! O not in vain
> We learned of old thy lowly strain.
> Fain in thy shadow would we rest
> And kneel with thee, and call thee blest.
> With thee would "magnify the Lord"
> And if thou art not here adored
> Yet seek we, day by day, the love and fear
> Which brings thee, with all Saints, near and more near.
> What glory thou above has now
> By special grace of thy dear Son,
> We see not yet, nor dare espy
> Thy crowned form with open eye. . .
> Therefore as kneeling day by day
> We to our Father duteous pray.
> So unforbidden may we speak
> An Ave to Christ's mother meek;
> (As children with "good morrow" come
> To elders in some happy home);
> Inviting so the saintly host above
> With our unworthiness to pray in love.

For its disinclination, amounting to scrupulous timidity, its furtive half accord and half demur, this poem is faint praise without parallel. In his second stanza (above), Keble manages to cast doubt on the doctrine of the Assumption; and in a later verse he seems —intentionally? — to undermine the doctrine of the Immaculate Conception in saying: "O awful station, to no seraph given/On this side touching sin, on the other heaven!" Keble ends by equating his greeting of the mother of God with a mundane salute daily given to all who might be construed as saintly. The thought is perhaps sound; its expression certainly falteringly hesitant. But that is the man, and his mode — saintly. (No saint is "saintly").

The doctrinal tradition re-emerged into consciousness in the work of the nineteenth century Tractarians, who preached a return to the Fathers and thus rediscovered the *Theotokos* as an inescapable prime datum. Both Keble and Pusey made their contributions, but it was Newman who took the Oxford movement's marian researches furthest, as much during the 1830s to his conversion in 1845 as during his long years as a Catholic. Looking back at the time of his conversion, he wrote: "I have ever been under the Blessed Virgin's shadow, if I may say it. My college was St Mary's, and my church, and when I went to Littlemore, there by my own previous disposition, Our Blessed Lady was waiting for me. Nor did she do nothing for me in that low habitation, of which I always think with pleasure."[11] He had preached on the feast of the Annunciation in 1832: "Who can estimate the holiness and perfection of her, who was chosen to be the mother of Christ? . . . What must have been the transcendent purity of her, whom the Creator Spirit condescended to overshadow with his miraculous presence? . . . What, think you, was the sanctified state of that human nature, of which God formed his sinless son?"[12] For his pains, Newman was accused by his fellows of holding the doctrine of Immaculate Conception. But this was no isolated sermon.[13]

In his last two Anglican years at Littlemore, Newman wrote his masterpiece, *An Essay on the Development of Christian Doctrine*, and in its pages (published at the hour of his conversion) is the fullest exposition of mariology for that whole period, from either of his two Churches. Newman found that in countries where Our Lady had been cherished, faith in the divinity of her son had not flagged.[14] He found in the Fathers the concept of Mary as the new and Second Eve, a view central thereafter to his marian thought. As early as in 1832, he had preached: "As in the beginning, woman was formed out of man by Almighty Power, so now, by a like mystery, but a reverse order, the new Adam was fashioned from the woman,"[15] This strong view he took into the centre of his *Letter to Pusey* (1866), his only mariological work. From this image he derived all her privileges, her holiness, her dignity, her being the Immaculate Conception, her divine motherhood, the power of her intercession, and more. Newman's mariology was not a morning mist, but has continued to be attended to. He was quoted by no less than Pope Pius XII on 4 May 1952, in the aftermath of his promulgating the dogma of the

Assumption, when he had this to say. "One dares not separate the mother from the son. His death on Golgotha was her martydom; his triumph is her exaltation. The witness of three centuries confirms the fact, as the learned Cardinal Newman pointedly observed, that Catholics who have honoured the mother, still worship the son... So with all the ardour of your faith, be quick at all times to offer to the Virgin Mother the homage of your gratitude, your love and your loyalty."[16]

Papal championship of a doctrine or spirituality is not always a guarantee of its prosperity. At the end of the last century, Leo XIII gave a decided impetus to the marian movement within the Catholic Church by several encyclicals emphasising Mary's intercessory power and stressing the value of prayer to her, particularly the rosary. Marian congresses first appeared in his reign and were taken futher in that of Pius X, who, to commemorate the fiftieth anniversary of the defining of the dogma of the Immaculate Conception, issued his encyclical *Ad diem illus* (February 1904), in which he declared that Christ was our Saviour and the origin of all the benefits of salvation *de condigno*, Mary could rightly be described as *reparatrix de congruo*. Benedict XV, preoccupied with the Great War, did not provide an encyclical, but he issued many statements that later mariologists found far from reserved. The year of the apparition at Fatima, 1917, also saw the foundation of Fr (now St) Maximilian Kolbe's "Militia of the Immaculate Conception", the first modern marian mass movement of two million members. In 1921 the Legion of Mary was founded in Dublin. In the 1930s more movements began, and more apparitions occurred, both emphasising Mary's intercessory power. A Maynooth professor has judged of it all, "In our day, as never before, devotional practices to the Blessed Virgin Mary seem to have become the typical form of Roman Catholic popular piety."[17] That would equally seem to be a far cry from ecumenical rapprochement; and indeed even such ecumenical luminaries as Cardinal Mercier of Malines were champions also of Mary as mediatrix of all graces (a doctrine that rightly died at the Council, despite fond hopes beforehand).

The reign of Pius XII from 1939 saw an astonishing — and, to wise eyes, worrying — upsurge in devotional practice, over-supported by a Pope who dreamed of an Age of Mary. He said more officially than his five predecessors, and more in his last retractive years than in the earlier expansive years. In 1950 he called the first International Marian Congress at Rome, defining the dogma of the Assumption that August. In 1954 he commemorated the centenary of the other dogmatic pro-mulgation of modern times by proclaiming a marian year and calling a second congress at Rome, afterwards in an encyclical proclaiming the Queenship of Mary. In his last year, 1958, he called a third congress, this time at Lourdes. All produced their Proceedings — the Lourdes one running to sixteen volumes. Indeed on average, during 1948-58, a thousand "scientific" marian works per year confronted the theologian, much of it from high places in Rome; and so many were the regional congresses that in 1954 alone they totalled more than forty. Devotional practices, meetings and institutes, writings and libraries all followed suit; and it went on into the 1960s, without thought for any ecumenical sensitivity.

Meanwhile there were stirrings in Anglicanism. A.T. Wirgman's classic of 1899, *The Blessed Virgin Mary and the Whole Company of Heaven*, well rooted in the ancient Anglican tradition and natural successor of Pusey's *Eirenicon* (1869), had quietly borne fruit down the years, not least in the writing of an exuberant Anglo-Catholic, Bede Frost, in the 1920s. One effect was that the Society of Mary, to promote devotion to Our Lady among Anglicans, was founded in 1931 (and now has the Bishop of London as its Superior General). Professor Eric Mascall, later to be a founder member of the Ecumenical Society of the Blessed Virgin Mary (ESBVM), gathered the team of fellow Anglicans and friendly Orthodox from the 1947 Conference of the Society of St Alban & St Sergius, editing a symposium entitled *The Mother of God* (London, 1949); and he went on, with an Anglican priest, Rev. H.S. Box, to edit a second collection of theological essays, *The Blessed Virgin Mary* (1963). In his latter preface, Dr Mascall wrote: "The Blessed Mother of the Lord has been badly neglected in recent Anglican theology . . . For the sake of the Anglican Com-munion and of Christendom as a whole, it is desirable that this neglect should be corrected." There was one clear exception to that judgement, Sir Edwyn Hoskyns' posthumous commentary on *The Fourth Gospel* (1940; he died in 1937), where he had shown clear parallels between Genesis 1-3 and the fourth gospel. Of Mary on Calvary, he wrote: "When the Fathers say that Mary is the new Eve, they had caught the meaning of the passage far better than modern commentators."[18] Hoskyns was alone among English Anglican or Protestant commentators in seeing her in a biblical context as the new Eve, as when he wrote of Calvary; "The mother of the Lord prefigures and foreshadows the Ecclesia of God. Mary, the mother of the Lord, becomes the mother of the faithful, and the beloved Disciple here seems to denote the ideal Christian convert."[19]

The Second Vatican Council: the decree on the Church, Lumen Gentium VIII

When the Council opened at Rome, the Anglicans were continuing to restore marian shrines (having begun restoring Lady Chapels since the mid-nineteenth century); while the Catholics were sated with mariology. What the Fathers did was most ecumenically delicate, to build in their Mary schema to the Church schema, she being of the Church and not above it; to return to the biblical and patristic sources alone found acceptable to many non-Catholics; and to propose phraseology that could not give offence to those who had increasingly feared extremism from Rome. Care is taken first to stress the unique mediator, Jesus Christ, and to show that were the unfortunate title "mediatrix" to be applied to Mary, it would be only in the sense that adds to the dignity and effectiveness of the one mediator.[20] The outcome has proven a profoundly important starting point for marian ecumenical dialogue, placing Mary rightly in Christian belief and practice. The Fathers well knew that the theological issues of God, man, sin, salvation, grace all run together and are thrown into sharpest focus by the theology of Mary; and that the ecumenical quarrel settles primarily on the nature of divine salvation rather than mariology, the marian dogmas being a facet of that larger issue.

It might be well to recall the five parts of the last chapter of *Lumen Gentium*, and to recall also that they represent the last words that the Fathers of the Council had to say about the Church.[21] The chapter begins with the role of the Blessed Virgin first in the mystery of Christ and the Church; and then in the economy of salvation. It goes on to the *esse* of and then

65

the devotion to, the Blessed Virgin in the Church. It ends by discussing Mary as "a sure sign of hope and solace for the People of God on pilgrimage." The last section begins thus: "It gives great joy and comfort to this holy Synod that among the separated brethren, too, there are those who give due honour to the mother of our Lord and Saviour. This is especially so among Eastern Christians, who with ardent fervour and heartfelt devotion assemble for the veneration of the ever virgin mother of God. Let the entire body of Christ's faithful pour forth their urgent prayers to the mother of God and mother of men."[22]

This schema should be near the heart of English ecumenists, for it had its genesis in the collaboration of two monks of Downside, one of whom was to become a leading figure in the first Anglican/Roman Catholic International Commission (ARCIC I). That was Dom Christopher Butler, Abbot of Downside and Abbot President of the English Benedictine Congregation, who became the Auxiliary Bishop of Westminster in December 1966: he was at the Council for all of its sessions with full voting rights as an Abbot President. His collaborator was Dom Ralph Russell, one of the founders of the ESBVM and a regular early contributor to its deliberations. On 5 October 1963, Abbot Butler wrote home: "I spent a busy day preparing a copy, for presentation to the Secretariat of the Council, of my (really Fr Ralph's) chapter on Our Lady — it has already been indicated that Our Lady might be put into the treatise on the Church (instead, I think, of having a treatise to herself). . . About the 'Downside' schema de BVM . . .", etc[23]. This background of *Lumen Gentium* VIII is further illuminated in a letter of an Ampleforth monk, Dom Henry Wansbrough, to his Abbey, written on 13 October 1963 from the Pontifical Biblical Institute in Rome:

> Ralph Russell (DD, Downside) produced a schema on mariology, which Abbot Butler has proposed with the support of the English hierarchy, to be substituted for the old schema —written early in 1962 — and to constitute an appendix, or a climax, to *De Ecclesia*. The reason for the enthusiasm is that it is based on Fr Ralph's doctoral thesis on St John Damascene (c750-60), plus Newman's *Letter to Pusey*. Hence it is very patristic, and quotes only what was said before the beginnings of most of today's

schisms in the Church. Hence it is both acceptable to all — instead of being a tissue of quotes from Pius XI — and especially apt to stand at the end of *De Ecclesia*. For, as you know, Mary and the Church is a chief theme of early mariology . . . The last page is a solid list of references to early Fathers. (Karl) Rahner said it is much the best proposed, better than those of (Cardinal) Suenens and (René) Laurentin, and he would propose only a very few minor changes. (Rahner has scarcely ever given such unqualified approval.)[24]

It was this same schema that made its way, after due public polishing, to its place at the end of the Dogmatic Constitution on the Church, promulgated on 21 November 1964. Again, within the millennium, English monks had taken a strong lead in the development of marian doctrine. One should add that Abbot Butler, like Newman, had found his theological training at Oxford in the Anglican Church: from St John's College (of which he is an Honorary Fellow) he took a First in Theology, and from Keble College he was studying for the priesthood in the Church of England in 1927.

The Anglican Roman Catholic International Commission (ARCIC I)[25]
The thaw between Rome and the worldwide Anglican Communion (composed of more than twenty-five mostly self-governing Churches, provinces or dioceses in loose federation or fellowship, i.e. *Koinonia*) had set in before the Council began. The clear milestones are these: first, the Resolutions of the ten-yearly Lambeth Conferences, of which the most influential was the 1920 Appeal for Christian Unity[26]; and secondly, the visits of the Archbishops of Canterbury to the Popes in the Vatican — reconnoitred in 1944 by William Temple (who died before he could do more); achieved as a "personal", rather than official, visit by Geoffrey Fisher to John XXIII in December 1960; triumphantly and officially achieved by Michael Ramsey to Paul VI in March 1966[27]; consolidated by Donald Coggan again to Paul VI in April 1977[28]; and reversed by Robert Runcie when he invited John Paul II to Canterbury in May 1982[29]. These events were punctuated by the establishment of the Secretariat for Promoting Christian Unity

(SPCU), under Cardinal Augustin Bea and Bishop Jan Willebrands, in 1960; SPCU's invitation of non-Catholic observers (the Anglican delegation, led by Bishop John Moorman, being the largest and most attentive) to the Council's plenary sessions; and the establishment in 1966 of the Anglican Centre in Rome. The two Communions were resolved to close the distance between themselves, and a Joint Preparatory Commission (the Anglicans being led by Bishop Moorman, fresh from writing his book, *Vatican Observed*) prepared the ground for ARCIC I[30], the Commission which produced four Agreed Statements on Eucharist (Windsor, 1971), Ministry (Canterbury, 1973), Authority I (Venice, 1976) and Authority II (Windsor, 1981). It was section 30 of the last which carried ARCIC's statement on mariology[31].

Among the ARCIC preparatory papers, there is very little of mariology. Very early on, in August 1970, a sub-commission on Church and Authority considered a paper presented by the Anglican Dr R.J. Halliburton (a consultant of the Commission) on "The Exercise of Authority: an Anglican Approach to the Dogmas of the Immaculate Conception and the Assumption"[32]. He began by saying that Anglicans, on hearing of papal pronouncements on matters of faith, suspected Rome of further corruption of the primitive faith: but he then provided assurance from the words of Newman and Maurice in the last century and Owen Chadwick and Ian Ramsey in this, that dogmatic statements are but the product of the Church articulating the faith she actually believes, and by which she lives; and reflecting on her past and present experience of life in the Redeeming Christ. He wrote of Anglican marian theology that it both stood as protest against seeming abuse and corruption in the late Middle Ages, and was inclined to adopt wholesale the Roman theology of Mary: the result has been too much "extraordinary" devotion, and not enough "ordinary" (though the 1662 Book of Common Prayer did reserve five feasts of the Virgin). The modern return to the patristic age in the theological study[33] has led to a reappraisal of Mary as the type of the Church, Mary as the beginning of our redemption and freedom from sin, and Mary as prefiguring in the salvation of her soul and body that of all the redeemed. With that approach, Dr Halliburton judged, a large measure of ecumenical agreement in faith can be reached: it requires that theology is taught first, that faith may be roused.

When ARCIC came to deal with problems of authority, prior to the 1976 Venice Agreed Statement, Père Jean Tillard, OP, (a member of the Commission) wrote a paper on *Sensus fidelium*[34]. Showing that it is, together with what the Church calls the unanimous consensus of the Fathers and Doctors, one of the major threads making up the fabric of tradition (and that is different from the meaning accorded by the Reformation communities), he took the two marian definitions of 1854 and 1950 as an example: "It — the *sensus fidelium* — is also, the use of vocabulary of Max Weber, the bearer of a conviction on which the Magisterium itself must draw when it feels the need to affirm the content of the faith in the most authoritative manner at its disposal" (p.5). Thus Pius IX, in his encyclical letter *Ubi primum* (1849), called on the bishops to inform him of the devotion of the clergy and faithful and what desire they had for the promulgation of a decree upon the Immaculate Conception. When in 1854 the Bull *Ineffabilis* was promulgated, it was the *perpetuus ecclesiae sensus* which carried the weight of the argument. Similarly in 1946 Pius XII, in his letter *Deiparae Virginis*, asked the bishops to tell him "what devotion the clergy and the people entrusted to their guidance show to the Assumption of the Sacred Virgin each in proportion to his faith and piety" and above all what they themselves, in union with their clergy and people, felt about a dogmatic definition on that point. The Pope justified his subsequent actions by the requests coming to him from the whole Christian people. His Bull *Munificentissimus Deus* (1950) constantly appealed to shared conviction of pastors and faithful, a conviction evident in the pressure from below favouring a solemn definition. The lived faith, the practical tradition, preceded the papal initiative to consult and then define: in both cases of marian definition, it was a *conspiratio antistitum et fidelium, consensus Christianorum, communis fides, universae ecclesiae fides*. The definition fixed a devotion which was a lived reality.

It might be well to bring to our minds the ARCIC mariological statement of 1981. The context is the two marian definitions — of 1854 and 1950 — as examples of dogmas promulgated by the Bishop of Rome outside a synod (i.e. non-collegially). Anglicans and Catholics found common agreement, in these dogmas, upon the one mediator between God and man, Mary's role never obscuring that affirmation about Jesus Christ. But Mary is inseparably linked with the doctrines of Christ and his Church; she has a unique vocation as *Theotokos*, and is most honoured in the communion of saints; "she was prepared by divine grace to be the mother of our Redeemer, by whom she herself was redeemed and received into glory", becoming "our model of holiness, obedience and faith", and "a prophetic figure of the Church of God before as well as after the Incarnation". All that is commonly agreed: there follows a curiously defensive footnote, which deserves to be in larger print, and must receive our notice:

> The affirmation of the Roman Catholic Church that Mary was conceived without original sin is based on recognition of her unique role within the mystery of the Incarnation. By being thus prepared to be the mother of our Redeemer, she also becomes a sign that the salvation won by Christ was operative among all mankind before his birth. The affirmation that her glory in heaven involves full participation in the fruits of salvation expresses and reinforces our faith that the life of the world to come has already broken into the life of our world. It is the conviction of Roman Catholics that the Marian dogmas formulate a faith consonant with Scripture.[35]

What is that, a unilateral statement which the Anglican members felt unable to sign? In the main text, there follows a strong Anglican "Nevertheless. . ." clause about the two marian definitions not being sufficiently supported by scripture, and their being unsuitably binding on all the faithful by the teaching authority of the Bishop of Rome, even though they had never been put to a Council. The Commission added: "One consequence of our separation has been a tendency for Anglicans and Roman Catholics alike to exaggerate the importance of the Marian dogmas in themselves at the expense of other truths more closely related to the foundation of the Christian faith."

All the signs of failed agreement are there, or at least a refusal of one side to accept the terms of the other's doctrinal utterance. It has been argued later by a member of ARCIC I and II, who is also a leading member of ESBVM, that common agreement can and must be found by the two extremes faring forward into the common ground between them[36]. If the Churches of the Reformation, inclined to reject the two marian dogmas of 1854 and 1950, will at least accept that they can be legitimate *theologoumena* (positions which may legitimately and freely be held without infidelity to the gospel, positions permissible but not essential); and, still more, if they will accept the truths underlying them as integral Christian faith concerning salvation, then there is hope. If the Church of Rome will then accept that this essential doctrine can and may also be expressed in non-marian terms, then the way may be open to agreement without either side renouncing a fundamental tradition. There is need for the theologians to *relire*, to redigest sectarian language so that it becomes expressive of the mind of the Church declaring itself; from which acceptance easily follows. Common ground may reside just outside our front gates!

The Ecumenical Society of the Blessed Virgin Mary (ESBVM)
The ESBVM was founded by a Catholic layman who had been an Anglican deacon, Martin Gillett, KCSG (d. 23 April 1980), from an inspiration gathered in conversation with Léon-Josef Cardinal Suenens, the Primate of Belgium, while attending a commemoration of the Halifax-Mercier Malines Conversations. Cardinal Heenan of Westminster and Bishop Allison of Winchester giving it a favourable wind, the Society was set up in 1967 "to advance the study at various levels of the place of the Blessed Virgin Mary in the Church, under Christ, and the related theological questions; and in the light of such study to promote ecumenical devotion"[37]. That professed aim was quickly and successfully promoted at various pastoral levels, theologians being asked always to play their part in sound teaching. This is not the place to relate the history of the Society to date, with its ten branches in Britain, and its foundations in the United States and in Ireland; nor to tell in detail of its six international congresses. Enough to say that the first at Coloma College, Kent, had Cardinal Suenens as its father figure in 1971, the main papers being published in pamphlet form. The two Presidents were Bishop Holland of Salford and Bishop Chadwick of Barking. At the second

congress in Birmingham in 1973, the two Presidents were Bishop Kenneth Sansbury (General Secretary of the British Council of Churches) and Bishop Alan Clark (President of the Ecumenical Commission of England & Wales, Co-Chairman of ARCIC I); there some remarkable papers were given from both sides of the Atlantic and across the Channel, the central paper coming from Abbé René Laurentin, "Mary and the Communion of Saints"[38] At the third in Birmingham in 1975, a message of goodwill came from the Cardinal Secretary of State, two Cardinals and the Archbishop of Canterbury; the proceedings being published in *The Way* (Supplement 25, 96pp), the central paper coming from Fr John McHugh of Durham, on "True Devotion to the Blessed Virgin"[39]. At the fourth at Westminster Cathedral and in Oxford in 1979, Cardinal Basil Hume had become the Society's President and gave an opening address; this being the last congress of Martin Gillett's life, Pope John Paul II sent him a signed personal letter blessing the Society's work. Proceedings were published in *One in Christ*[40]. By the time of the fifth at Canterbury in 1981, Archbishop Robert Runcie had become a Co-President, and was sad at having to ask the Bishop of Dover to deputise for him at the final Eucharist in the Cathedral; the Proceedings were again published in *The Way* (Supplement 45, 96pp). At the sixth congress in Dublin in 1984, a new dimension was offered in the three main papers and seven "communications" provided from an Irish provenance. But still, as on all previous congresses, a strong and strongly contributive contingent flew across the Atlantic and some scholars made their way from the Continent; the proceedings were again published by *The Way* (Supplement 6, 96pp)[41]. Cardinal Suenens, who had been the father of Canterbury, had by then become our Patron, with the Bishop of London and the former President of the Methodist Conference (Dr John Newton), and was content to send his prayers[42].

The Society's activities are not encompassed by branch meetings, prayer events and pilgrimages and by the International Congresses. An account of the Society's work during 1980-84[43], besides dealing briefly with structures and personalities, tells of the various publications. Of these, pride of place must go to a collection of the more significant papers not already published in *The Way* or *One in Christ*: that means that the 280 pages of papers are drawn in the main from those given at branch meetings, AGMs, the Autumn one-day conference on non-congress years and other conferences. They range widely, into the religious world beyond Christianity as well as into the theology of Luther, Zwingli, Calvin and other Protestant positions, all as related to the Blessed Virgin and the problems raised by her place in Christian dialogue[44]. Meanwhile papers are steadily delivered and the best regularly published: of these, one of the most remarkable was from Fr John McHugh, "*Theotoke* the earliest known invocation of the mother of God", a study of the Rylands papyrus, 470, of the prayer that appeared in the earliest Latin as *Sub tuum praesidium*, dated by the great Lobel on palaeographic grounds as pre-300, that is, before the conciliar definition of *Theotokos*. Weekend joint meetings with other societies, such as the Catholic Eastern (Uniate) Society of St John Chrysostom to study "The Mother of God in Eastern Theology and Spirituality", have been held and judged a lively and valuable interplay. The Society, conscious that it inclines to a bilateral dialogue between Anglicans and Catholics, had continued to seek out involvement from the Free Churches (a Methodist minister in London being our liturgical secretary) and the Orthodox Churches (Bishop Kallistos of Diokleia, Spalding Lecturer in Eastern Orthodox Studies at Oxford, being one of our more participatory lecturing members): it is, in this manner, four-legged and in need of all four — although the three episcopal Executive Co-Chairmen do not include a member from the Orthodox tradition as yet.

Conclusion and concluding survey

On 22 March 1974 Paul VI promulgated a ninety page document for the renewal of devotion to the Blessed Virgin, *Marialis cultus*.[45] He commended that devotion to the virgin should be imbued with the great themes of the Christian message and have a biblical imprint; that it should harmonise with the spirit of the liturgy; that it should reflect the deepest concerns of the Church, especially Christian unity. He said: "Devotion to the humble handmaid of the Lord. . . will become, even if only slowly, not an obstacle but a path and a rallying point for the union of all who believe in Christ. We are glad to see that in fact a better understanding of Mary's place in the mystery of Christ and of the Church on the part also of our separated brethren is smoothing the path to union" (n. 33). After speaking of unity in marian devotion with the Orthodox, the Pope went on: "Catholics are also united with Anglicans, whose classical theologians have already drawn attention to the sound scriptural basis for devotion to the mother of our Lord, while those of the present day increasingly underline the importance of Mary's place in the Christian life. Praising God with the very words of the virgin, they are united too with their brethren in the Churches of the Reform, where love for the sacred scriptures flourishes" (n. 32). The Pope went on: "The ecumenical aspect of marian devotion is shown in the Catholic Church's desire that, without in any way detracting from the unique character of this devotion, every care should be taken to avoid any exaggeration which could mislead other Christian brethren from the true doctrine of the Catholic Church" (ibid). Such a sentiment, with its relation to those beyond Rome, could not have been expressed twenty years earlier: thus far had the Churches travelled.

Many were the bilateral and religional dialogues, and some of them took in mariology fruitfully. Of these, let us select one to stand for all — the United States dialogue between the Catholic Bishops' Committee for Ecumenical and Inter-religious Affairs and the National Committee of the Lutheran World Federation (now Lutheran World Ministries). Since the end of the Council in 1965, theologians from both of those traditions have produced joint statements on the creed, Baptism, the Eucharist, the ministry, papal primacy, Peter in New Testament and then Mary in New Testament (studied between 1975-8).[46] As to the last, a study group of two Lutherans and two Catholics made a presentation of their findings to a plenary group of twelve in an elaborate series of sessions. The studies drew on non-canonical, patristic and Gnostic sources, as well as Old Testament passages and themes, being redrafted by other groups. They commented later: "The interchange opened new horizons for all, so that the end product was achieved not so much by way of compromise or concession, but by way of mutual and creative discovery." They all found that they shared a common regard for the mother of Jesus (as the fourth gospel always calls her); they learned what faith and discipleship ought to mean within the family of God. What they offered, as their assessment of Mary, was a collective study truly representative of the whole group. "The norm was not total agreement, but a consensus about reasonable limits of plausibility."[47]

Bilateral conversations, with their joint reports, were one step away from what has occurred since, unofficial enthusiastic congress, "ecumenical declarations". They are found in marian congresses, as in others. One such occurred at the congress in October 1979 at Zaragoza in Spain (held immediately after the ESBVM congress, and timed so that those who attended one might go on to the next). The declaration read thus:

> . . . in this eighth International Mariological Congress. . ., a group of Orthodox, Anglican, Lutheran and Reformed theologians have met with their Catholic brethren. . . [and] discovered many common elements in their approach to the mother of God, more indeed than they could have expected. They feel able to formulate these convictions in the following way:
>
> The problem of the *invocation* and *intercession* of Mary was examined afresh in this congress. We have considered it against the background of the communion of saints. As a Christian can and should pray for others, we believe that the saints who have already entered into the fullness which is in Christ, amongst whom Mary holds the first place, can and do pray for us sinners who are still suffering and struggling on earth. The one and unique mediation of Christ is in nothing affected by this. The meaning of the direct invocation of the saints who are alive in God, an invocation which is not practised in all the Churches, remains to be elucidated.[48]

Such a statement is most heartening, but in some ways alarming; for it cuts across lines of authentic magisterium and sets up ad hoc congresses, particularly composed of charismatic and influential — but not necessarily responsible — theologians, as a new teaching or proclaiming factor, influence without responsibility. There is a Protestant principle afoot here, unless it is ultimately submissive to the formal magisterium of the Churches concerned. Here is a new elan of the Spirit, the charismatic come to the theologian; and it requires discipline.[49]

The matter is not a single event, or of the past. At a mariological congress held in Malta during September 1983, a similar group of theologians made a further ecumenical declaration, equally heartening. They took up from the one reported above, saying that "There is no reason preventing us, even with our confessional differences, from uniting our prayer to God in the Spirit with the prayer of the heavenly liturgy, and especially with the prayer of the mother of God."[50] It is a good place to end this paper, though it is not an end but a new and further beginning, far removed from the distrust of earlier centuries. We are all heirs to good will.

Postscript

Even as winter writing ends, spring encroaches with its crop of seeds, three of which — because of their significance — have to be further noticed. the first is a book by the chairman of the Canterbury branch of the Ecumenical Society of the BVM, Canon A. M. Allchin, *The Joy of all Creation: An Anglican Meditation on the Place of Mary* (DLT, 1984). In some ways it is a return to old ground, such as his 1978 explorations in Christian spirituality, in the writings of Lancelot Andrewes, Jeremy Taylor, Mark Frank, Thomas Traheme, Euros Bowen, Edwin Muir or T. S. Eliot. In other ways it has a newness of approach: for instance, in Eliot he has found a mariology, mostly concentrated in "The Dry Salvages", especially in the fourth section, which even quotes from Dante's *Paradiso*, "*Virgine madre, figlia del tuo figlio*" (daughter of your own Son) —

> Lady, whose shrine stands on the promontory, pray for all those who are in ships . . . Repeat a prayer also on behalf of women who have seen their sons or husbands setting forth, and not returning . . . Pray for those who were in ships and ended their voyage . . . wherever cannot reach them the sound of the sea bell's perpetual angelus.
> (Perpetual intercession from the mother of God)

In his epilogue, Canon Allchin has highlighted the recovery of the marian shrine at Walsingham, to which flock in ever increasing numbers Anglicans and other Christians of conviction.

Who would have believed at the beginning of this century

that Walsingham would again become a national centre of pilgrimage, and a place of great ecumenical influence, attracting Roman Catholics and Orthodox, as well as Anglicans and Christians of other traditions? Who in the early years of Fr Hope Patten's pioneering struggle to restore the shrine would have believed that within fifty years an Archbishop of Canterbury would again come to Walsingham, and would preach and preside at the great Whitsuntide pilgrimage? (p. 156).

That was in May 1980; and since then the Anglican Archbishop and the Cardinal of Westminster have both made a pilgrimage to that same shrine. So does marian ecumenism continue to unfold.

The second is Pope John Paul II's initiative in asking Catholic bishops throughout the world to consecrate that world to the Immaculate Heart of Mary, using the prayer: "We have recourse to your protection, holy mother of God." In 1944 and again in 1954 Pius XII did no less than that. This Pope, who attributes his survival after his attempted assassination to the prayers of the mother of God, in early February had this to say: "The power of this consecration lasts for all time and embraces all individuals, peoples and nations. It overcomes every evil that the spirit of darkness is able to waken, and has in fact awakened in our times, in the heart of man and in his history . . . In entrusting to you, O mother, the world, all individuals and peoples, we also entrust to you this very consecration of the world, placing it in your motherly heart. . . ." It has been noticed that the Pope's words are practically the same as those he used at Fatima in May 1982; they were to be promulgated on the Feast of the Annunciation, the anniversary of the beginning of the Holy Year of the Redemption.

The third is the newest of the "mariophanies" around the world, Medjugorje in Yugoslavia. During autumn 1988, across a period of several weeks, it was reported that the concrete cross above the village regularly disappeared to be replaced by the figure of Our Lady, a phenomenon that was seen and shared by the whole community of villagers. Two pilgrims from Argyllshire, Ruth MacFarlane-Barrow and Kenneth Black, took themselves to the village for the New Year, and wrote (*Catholic Herald*, 10 February 1984, p. 5): "As for the apparitions themselves, we were present on two consecutive evenings while the children were in ecstacy; we found this deeply and spiritually moving." They remarked that the most startling of revelations had been that the Blessed Virgin said that this was to be the last time she would appear on earth: the visionary Maria Pavlovic stressed this in an interview. The whole "event" appears to be ordered to peace — first peace within the person and the family, without which they are in a weak position to promote peace beyond themselves; and then by degrees throughout the world. This can best be attained through personal prayer and fasting, and regular attendance at the sacrament of Penance.

All of these, the book, the Holy Father's dedication and the newest mariophany, have ecumenical implications for better or for worse. The book may confirm Anglican mariology in a historico-literary context and present it as such to a wider world with stronger and welcoming traditions of marian thought and practice; the papal dedication may even prove an obex to ecumenical progress, judged to be a return to nineteenth century frames of thought and devotion; and the experiences coming from Medjugorje may appear to some as weird, to others as proof positive of Mary's solicitude — and claim to our attention.

5

ANGLICANS AND MARY: A CHURCH OF IRELAND RESPONSE TO THE PAPER OF DOM ALBERIC STACPOOLE, OSB

Very Reverend John Paterson

For some the search for a relationship between members of the Anglican Communion and the Blessed Virgin Mary must appear to have the same level of realisation as the discovery of a Presbyterian bishop or a white blackbird! However, I understand that white blackbirds can exist (even if only as albinos). I am aware of at least one Presbyterian bishop (from the United Church of North India but now retired home to his Irish Presbyterian church). And I know that Anglicanism, when it has been truest to the teaching of its Book of Common Prayer, has always had a doctrine of the Communion of Saints of which the Blessed Virgin is the first and foremost member.

This Anglican approach to Our Lady has been developed by Dom Alberic in his paper with great sensitivity. He has been both ecumenically generous and ecumenically realistic. Indeed because of his approach it almost goes against the grain to have to differ from him at all! Yet differ I must on the question of the Thirty Nine Articles.

First of all I must make clear that the Thirty Nine Articles are not *the* doctrine of the Church of Ireland — only a part of it. To the Articles must be added the Book of Common Prayer and the services for the Ordering of Bishops, Priests and Deacons. Liturgy too is a constituent part of doctrine. But even were the Articles the sole doctrine of the Church of Ireland I think Dom Alberic is perhaps less than fair to them.

Article VI, I would suggest, is no hindrance to marian devotion. I agree, however, that it is an obstacle to marian doctrinal definition since it denies to holy tradition the status of an *independent* source of Christian teaching separate from scripture. For Anglicans holy tradition explains and amplifies the teaching of scripture; it is the Church's reflection on scripture from the days of the early Fathers to the theologians of today; but for us it cannot be a source of doctrine *independent* of scripture. And that, for me, is all that Article VI is saying.

Nor can I agree that Article XV is aimed against the doctrine of the Immaculate Conception. You cannot, in 1571, fire a missile at something that is not made *de fide* until 1854! But the very wording itself cannot be made to refer to Mary in any way. Referring to the sinlessness of Christ alone it describes everyone else (although baptised and born again in Christ) as offending in many things and that if we say we have no sin the truth is not in us. But wait, Our Lady was never "baptised and born again in Christ" so this can hardly be taken as a reference to her. The Articles are rarely less than straightforward in their attack on views they don't accept; they are never oblique; that was never sixteenth century practice on either side of the divide!

Article XXII is most certainly aimed at the corruption of the medieval religious tradition. On all sides now it can be acknowledged that there had existed widespread fraud and lucrative miracle-mongering and it had to be condemned; as in this quotation:

> Not that any Divinity or virtue is believed to be in them on account of which they are to be worshipped: or that anything is to be sought of them: or that trust is to be placed in images. . . . In the invocation of saints, the veneration of relics and the sacred use of relics let all superstition be taken away, all base gain be abolished, finally all lasciviousness be avoided, so that images be not painted or adorned in wanton beauty and men misuse not the celebration of saints and visitation of relics to revellings and drunkenness.

And that quotation, incidentally, is from Session 25 of the Council of Trent.

Article XXII certainly is tough and uncompromising in its language. It believed things were wrong in the Church and it said so. But, unlike Trent, it produced no anathemas. Controversy today has reached more civilised levels — we can now agree to disagree without being disagreeable. But even admitting this, is it fair to condemn the Articles, issued in 1571, for the destruction of Walsingham and other centres, which in fact had taken place in earlier decades of the century? But Dom Alberic is characteristically generous when he writes:

> Once the noise of denominational battle was stilled and a more reflective period was ushered in, once the Anglican Church had become sufficiently settled to allow of confident reflection, the seventeenth century interpreters of the faith often displayed a wistfulness towards the old marian devotion.

This new mariology, however, he describes as 'historico-literary' in style. In one sense, I suppose, this would be inevitable in a religious Communion which, until comparatively recent years, maintained no marian centres or shrines. Devotion — especially lay devotion — needs the outward and visible sign to feed the inward and spiritual faith.

Yet 'historico-literary' is also a little unfair. Anglican theology has always been highly incarnational in direction. So, it is noteworthy that most of the marian paeans of praise of seventeenth and eighteenth century Anglican writers occur in sermons on her son or about the sacraments which are regarded as extensions of the incarnation. We meet Mary through her son, a position probably acceptable to most Anglicans. For no Anglican liturgy, ancient or modern, contains a direct invocation to the Blessed Virgin or to any saint. The individual Anglican is left perfectly free to ask God for the prayers of those who have gone before him in the faith (and like the Orthodox we would not limit it just to canonised saints). The issue is one of pious belief, not Christian revelation, for us, and inclusion within the official liturgy would change that situation. It would be to affirm what scripture has not clearly affirmed and to deny liberty to those who felt unable to accept the claims upon which the practice is based.

For the remainder of this paper I want to leave you with two approaches to Anglican marian writing. Firstly that of the Church of England; secondly that of the Church of Ireland.

The Church of England
The Church of England has always maintained that the

English Reformation was more of an evolution than a revolution, that while the bathwater was let down the drain the baby was not thrown out with it. Yet it has to be admitted that all or nearly all the externals of Catholic devotion were swept away at the time of the Reformation and have only gradually been restored over the past one hundred and fifty years. The principals of the reformers were:

All glory is to God.
All grace is from God.
There is but one mediator between God and man, the man Christ Jesus.

And Anglicans would say that these principles must still be faced if doctrine and devotion are not to be divisive. Yet the remarkable thing in Reformation Anglicanism was that, even though the shrines were demolished and outward devotion ceased, Mary's role in the schema of salvation was still recognised. For Anglicans still recognised the decrees of the first four General Councils of the undivided Church as binding — including Ephesus and *Theotokos*. Despite this, resorting to Mary in prayer is not something that they would have practised or advocated. George Bull, bishop of St David's, made the point traditional to Anglican belief in the Communion of Saints, that we must never allow God's kingdom to be divided into one of justice (presided over by Jesus) and one of mercy (presided over by Mary). At the period it may not have been an unnecessary protest. Likewise William Forbes, bishop of Brechin in Scotland, distinguished between invocation of the saints which asked for their prayers and invocation which asked for their mercy. The former, asking God for their prayers, he believed to be both primitive and edifying.

John Jewel, Bishop of Salisbury, obviously had some of the more exotic writings of the medieval authors in mind when he said:

They do not only wickedly, but also shamefacedly, call upon the Blessed Virgin, Christ's mother, to have her remember that she is the mother, and to command her son, and to use a mother's authority over him.

Few today, probably, would regard his condemnation of such a position as being unduly harsh.

More conservative views among the reformers were held by Richard Hooker, Bishop of Salisbury and the greatest English theologian of his day. He followed the Dominican tradition which denied a doctrine of the Immaculate Conception, but he was a staunch defender of the title *Theotokos* because he saw it safeguarded the divinity of Christ.

These, then, were the views of some of the first and second generation of Reformation Anglican theologians. It has been said, and probably rightly, that they are better remembered for the faith they affirmed, than for the faith of others that they denied. But then is this not something that was true on both sides of the Reformation divide at the period?

Dom Alberic rightly reminds us that when the noise of denominational battle was silenced, a more reflective period in Anglicanism began. By the time of this third generation of Anglicans, the seventeenth century was well established, England was under no threat from Catholic Europe, and Anglican theology was free to develop along its own lines. One must, however, beware of treating the Caroline Divines as if they were infallible (as Anglican Catholics have tended to do) or else as Romanists in disguise (as Anglican evangelicals have suggested). They were neither.

Perhaps for the benefit of any who may not be totally familiar with Anglican theology I should say that it has always been made up of both Catholic and Puritan tendencies and, at different times, first one and then the other will tend to prevail. The seventeenth century was the first great period of Caroline Catholicism though it was rudely interrupted by Cromwell and the Puritans for nearly twenty years.

Yet even the most Catholic of Caroline Anglicans must have been somewhat taken aback when Anthony Stafford published *The Female Glory* with its imprimatur from Archbishop Laud. For here was no simple devotion on the life of Mary, but a document manifesting the most extravagant exuberances of baroque imagination. But it was not representative, and Stafford was no theologian.

From this period of English history it would be easy for me to string together a catena of quotations which might seem to demonstrate a deep mariological faith within the Church of England. But it would be false and it would be wrong of me to attempt it. Marian devotion certainly did exist in the minds and prayers of thinkers and scholars. But, as I have already said, it was probably non-existent for the ordinary man in the pew whose theology is usually based on what he can see. And nothing in his parish church, apart from some stained glass, would have let him see much of the Blessed Virgin Mary at this period!

But for the scholar the role of Mary in salvation history did exist and was important. Thomas Ken was one of the best known episcopal writers of the period. He was bishop of Bath and Wells during the reigns of both Charles II and James II. His marian piety is remarkably rich in its devotion. Indeed his poem for the first Sunday after the Epiphany is almost a life of the Virgin and one that even appears to proclaim both the Immaculate Conception and the Assumption — until one remembers that in his day both were still pious beliefs and not *de fide* doctrines.

> Her virgin-eyes saw God Incarnate born
> When she to Bethlehem came that happy morn.
> How high her raptures then began to swell,
> None but her own omniscient Son can tell;
> As Eve when she her fontal sin review'd,
> Wept for herself, and all she should include;
> Bless'd Mary, with man's Saviour in embrace,
> Joy'd for herself, and for all human race;
> The Holy Ghost his temple in her built,
> Cleansed from congenial, kept from mortal guilt,
> And from the moment that her blood was fired,
> Into her heart celestial love inspired.
> All saints are by her son's dear influence bless'd,
> She kept the very fountain at her breast;
> The son adored and nursed by the sweet maid,
> A thousand-fold of love for love repaid;
> Heaven with transcendent joys her entrance graced,
> Next to his throne her son his mother placed;
> And here below, now she's of heaven possessed
> All generations are to call her blessed.

For all this, Ken is yet strictly theological in his devotion. To find a more warm and personal devotion to the virgin we actually have to go back to the pre-Cromwellian period and to one who only in recent years has been rediscovered from obscurity. Mark Frank was a Fellow of Pembroke College, Cambridge. He was no radical who held unpopular views, but was indeed marked out for high promotion within the Church of England had not his early death occurred.

In his sermons preached in his beautiful college chapel he shows us the humble virgin as the mother of God, the type of the Church, and Christ's presence within her as related to his continuing presence in the life of the Church. For him she had indeed a true part in the mystery of the incarnation.

Preaching on a Christmas Day on Luke 2:2, "She brought forth her first-born son, and wrapped him in swaddling clothes, and laid him in a manger", his sermon begins abruptly with a shout of praise and thanksgiving:

> I shall not need to tell you who this 'she' or who this 'him'. The day rises with it in its wings. This day wrote it with the first ray of the morning sun upon the posts of the world. The angels sung it in their choirs, the morning stars together in their courses. The virgin mother, the eternal son. The most blessed among women, the fairest of the sons of men. The woman clothed with the sun, the sun compassed with a woman. She the gate of heaven, he the King of Glory that came forth. She the mother of the everlasting God: he God without a mother; God blessed for ever more. Great persons as ever met upon a day.
>
> Yet as great as the persons, and great as the day, the great lesson of them both is to be little, to think and make little of ourselves; seeing the infinite greatness in this day become so little, eternity a child, the rays of glory wrapt in rags, heaven crowded into the corner of a stable, and he that is everywhere want a room.

In his sermon for the feast of the Annunciation his previously oblique references to the role of Mary become more explicit. Puritan neglect of Mary demand his outspokenness:

> Nor should I scarce, I confess, have chosen such a theme today, though the gospel reach it me, but that I see it is time to do it, when Our Lord is wounded through Our Lady's sides; both Our Lord and the mother of Our Lord, most vilely spoken of by a new generation of wicked men, who, because the Romanists make little less of her than a goddess, they make not so much of her as a good woman;

because they bless her too much, these unbless her quite, at least will not suffer her to be blessed as she should.

What then is the main theme of the sermon? The angel's salutation gives it to us: "The Lord is with thee." Here is the heart of the matter. She is his mother; but he is her Lord. Yet he goes on to assert Mary's unique privilege and her unique place in the work of the gospel in a passage that gathers together the traditional titles and interpretations of her name:

> Maria is *maris stella* says St Bede: "the star of the sea"; a fit name for the mother of the bright Morning Star that rises out of the vast sea of God's infinite and endless love. Maria, the Syriac interprets *Domina*, "a lady", a name yet retained and given to her by all Christians; Our Lady, or the Lady mother of Our Lord. Maria, rendered by Petrus Damiani, *de monte et altitudine Dei*, highly exalted, as you would say, like the mountain of God, in which he would vouchsafe to dwell, after a more miraculous manner than in very Sion, his "own holy mount". St Ambrose interprets it, *Deus ex genere meo*, "God of my kin"; as if by her very name she was designed to have God born of her, to be *Deipara*, as the Church, against all heretics, has ever styled her, the mother of God.

Theologically his sermon reaches its climax in discussing *kecharitomene* (highly favoured/full of grace). For Frank the blessedness of Our Lady is God's pure grace, and it is noteworthy in his sermon that he nowhere uses the term merit. In this sense he definitely sits on the Reformation side of the controversy. For him grace is *favor Dei* rather than *gratia infusa*, yet having asserted the primacy of *favor Dei*, he can then serenely equate them.

As so often at the end of his sermons, he turns to speak of the sacrament about to be celebrated, and thus to the climax of his whole exposition: Christ's presence in the flesh through the child-bearing of blessed Mary, as the foundation of his presence in the Church, in each Christian, and particularly in the holy Eucharist, the focal point of the whole mystery of God's living presence among his people.

Yet not to such at any time more fully than in the

blessed Sacrament to which we are now a-going. There he is strangely with us, highly favours us, exceedingly blesses us; there we are all made blessed Marys, and become mothers, sisters and brothers of our Lord, whilst we hear his word, and conceive it in us; whilst we believe him who is the Word, and receive him too into us. There angels come to us on heavenly errands, and there our Lord indeed is with us, and we are blessed, and the angels hovering all about us to peep into those holy mysteries, think us so, call us so. There graces pour down in abundance on us — there grace is in its fullest plenty, —there his highest favours are bestowed upon us — there we are filled with grace unless we hinder it, and shall hereafter in the strength of it be exalted into glory — there to sit down with this blessed Virgin and all the saints and angels, and sing praise, and honour, and glory, to the Father, Son, and Holy Ghost, for ever and ever.

Because of these lengthy extracts, I still feel I must remind you that they must be set alongside much negative polemical literature and an almost total popular neglect of Mary. But it is *not* nothing, and it reveals that the writers quoted did not intend, any more than I believe did the reformers, to destroy the *whole* traditional veneration of Mary. What they attempted and hoped to do was to purify and question certain aspects of mariology, not to destroy it.

Eighteenth century Anglicanism went through an arid period of theology which, somewhat strangely, is known as "The Enlightenment" — almost a contradiction in terms. In the same century European Catholicism saw a flowering and growth of a new baroque mariology.

It was the late nineteenth century and the second phase of the Oxford Movement that reintroduced visible marian devotion into the Church of England. Statues appeared in churches up and down the country — sadly most of them cheap Italian plaster models. It was an age within the Anglo-Catholic movement that reckoned if a thing was Italian it must be right.

The twentieth century, as Dom Alberic has shown, has seen the fullest flowering of the age of Mary within the Church of England — though not without the opposition of the representatives of the old puritan tradition, always suspicious of change. Walsingham has been restored for some fifty years, and not only has Archbishop Runcie presided at the Whit Monday ceremonies, but, more significantly, the evangelical bishop of Norwich, in whose diocese it lies, has also been a visitor.

And of course one of the new classic marian writers was also an evangelical Anglican. I refer to John de Satgé whose sad death occurred in 1980. From his first foray into the subject 'way back in 1963 — somewhat like testing the sea on a cold day with your big toe — to his full length *Mary and the Christian Gospel* in 1976, still, he maintains, he writes within the evangelical tradition. There he even posits *a* doctrine of the Immaculate Conception, disliking what he regards as the unfortunate legal language of Pius IX (as do the Orthodox), and yet saying that it is capable of being understood in a way which can help us to know more fully the mystery of Christ, human and divine.

The Church of Ireland

So much for the Church of England. Now we move nearer home and to the Church of Ireland. "Well, that won't take us long", some of you may be thinking!

But many people only know the Church of Ireland perhaps through attendance at some ecumenical service — and such occasions are always planned to avoid giving offence to anyone! Television viewing, watching the eucharistic worship of other Churches within our own homes, has possibly done more for ecumenism than artificial ecumenical services. For it has shown each how the other *really* worships. I have known many somewhat bitter Protestants to take a completely different attitude to the Mass after they have actually seen it on the box. It wasn't what they thought and feared it to be. So too, I have at times had to refrain from laughing out when a Roman Catholic man or woman has said: "You actually have the Lord's Prayer and the Eucharist"! Yes, our ignorance of each other can still reach those lengths in some places.

Yet suspicions do remain. The average Church of Ireland person is, to say the least, uncomfortable if he visits Knock. It is not his ambience or environment and he feels lost. Mary, he knows, is the chief of the saints; he knows too that his Church uses the Magnificat, Mary's great song, every day at Evensong; he knows that four holy days are devoted to her honour during the year; and his wife will probably be a member of the Mothers' Union, a devotional guild based on the humility and childbearing of Mary. Yet none of this, of course, brings either of them into a personal relationship with Mary in the way that Knock does.

To admit such things, to admit that both our Churches have never taken the trouble seriously to understand what the other believes, could be a real breakthrough. "This is what *I* believe; now you tell me *your* faith." This was the method behind ARCIC as described by Dom Alberic. We have done it with selected delegates at high-level conferences. But we have left it undone at the local level. And it is not just a sin of omission; with Ireland in the condition we have known it since 1968, anything that is not done, when it could or ought to have been, must be laid at our feet as a deliberate sin of what we in Ireland sometimes call "letting well enough alone". And both our Churches have been guilty of it. Both in effect have said, "Ah, sure we're very nice to them nowadays (whichever 'they' are); we always invite them to special things; but we don't have to start living with them, do we?"

And of course, in a sense the answer is "Yes". If one can take the analogy of marriage; it's generally as the husband and wife grow into each other that they can come first to tolerate each other's difficult ways, and then come to learn why the other thinks the way he/she does — to learn to disagree without being disagreeable.

Here I have to say, in all charity, yet I believe in all honesty, that ecumenism in this land must be given its lead and given its head by you who are members of the Roman Catholic Church. You represent 75% of the Irish people on this island; indeed in some parts of the south and west this can reach nearly 100%. As your joy in this must be great, so too your duty to your separated brothers and sisters must be equally great. I know many of you will feel that your burden in education and among our rapidly expanding young population is already almost more than you can bear. But ecumenism, too, is not just a friendly option; it is a command of the Lord.

Perhaps because of your very size you have never known what it feels like to be in a church or a hall, lost in a vast sea of those who are not of your own tradition. Perhaps because of your numbers you have never experienced the hurt of being cut off from the sacraments of your own Church and told that you really ought not to receive; but of course it would have been very different if you hadn't said who you were! Our lack of ecumenism in the early years of this century have provided us with a legacy of bitterness that we are now reaping in full.

And we see it in our different mariologies. The Roman Catholic approach to Mary is warm and affectionate. Because of suspicions about this our Church of Ireland approach is often clinical and cerebral: we will talk *about* her, but not *to* her! Yet, as within the Church of England, there is a definite marian theology. It may be less developed but it is there and it is *not* nothing. So let us examine it.

The earliest reference I can find is from James Ussher, Archbishop of Armagh in the first half of the seventeenth century. On the subject of the invocation of the saints, he maintained that in the ancient Church their prayers were requested as fellow servants; invocation was not attributed as part of the worship due to them.

Jeremy Taylor, Bishop of Down from 1660-1667, was always regarded as a moderate. It cannot be said that he had a deep mariological understanding. Normally he speaks of Mary's past in the mystery of the Incarnation, but he can also see her as the model for every Christian which must suggest at least some sort of relationship.

And not until the present century can I discover another Church of Ireland writing on Mary. But now, actually, more interesting material is to be found.

Dr Kathleen Lynn was a daughter of the rectory. She was founder of St Ultan's hospital in Dublin and was surgeon-general to the Irish citizen army in the 1916 rising. Besides being a doctor she was also something of an amateur theologian. She writes on one occasion of her fear that if the Roman Catholic Church of her time continued to heap honour upon the Blessed Virgin then they could actually endanger the doctrine of the Incarnation by de-humanising the virgin. Dom Alberic has shown us this very danger at the time. Here we have it from a Church of Ireland laywoman and written at a time when many in her own Church would have equated mariology with mariolatry.

Next, and more importantly, let me introduce you to Archbishop John Gregg, Archbishop of Armagh from 1939-1959. As a student I well remember him in the late 1950s at meetings of the Anglican and Eastern Churches Association — accompanied by a tall and distinguished (though then beardless) archimandrite, now Archbishop Anthony with us today. Gregg was rector of Blackrock, Cork, about 1914, and got caught up, as so often then happened, in inter-Church controversy. It was an unhappy period when pamphlets told you more of what another Church did *not* believe than how much it shared with your own belief.

Gregg's book is called *The Primitive Faith and Roman Catholic Developments.* His marian chapter is expressed with fairness of language that only illustrates the greatness of the man. One need hardly say that he defended with sound biblical argument what he described as "the old Church tradition that the mother of the Lord remained in perpetual virginity". But let him speak for himself.

I am far from wishing to speak in any but the most respectful way of the mother of the Lord. All generations must call her blessed... She was "highly favoured among women". She holds the position which from the beginning to the end of time could be held by one woman alone. Only once could God be made man therefore only once could woman be the mother of the Incarnate God.

It is this unique position that St Mary fills. Upon this pure virgin rested the choice of heaven. With humble obedience she bowed her head and accepted her high and yet misunderstood office: "Behold the handmaid of the Lord, be it done unto me according to thy word". Who shall venture to measure the inspiration that was vouchsafed to the mother of the Lord? You know how close is the relation between the mother and the unborn child. You know that the mother's interests and thoughts and feelings impress themselves indelibly upon the babe in her womb. What spiritual protection and governance then must have been granted to the mother of the Lord...

It was not only of the sinless conception of the Saviour but also of the time between conception and nativity that those mysterious words were spoken by the angel: "The

91

Holy Ghost shall come upon thee and the power of the Highest shall over-shadow thee, therefore also that holy thing which shall be born of thee shall be called the Son of God".

No wonder then that we think of the Blessed Virgin as alone among women — alone in her privilege, alone in her special inspiration. It is quite easy to see how Irenaeus contrasted her with Eve and wrote: "Mary being obedient became to all mankind the cause of salvation". "The knot of Eve's disobedience was loosed by Mary's obedience". "As by a virgin the human race had been given over to death, so by a virgin it is saved".

Furthermore we need not object to the title "mother of God" provided we understand that the title was given her . . . to safeguard the doctrine of God the son. It means that she was mother after the flesh of him who is at once both God and man.

Let me now introduce you to my last and most recent Church of Ireland writer on mariology. Like so many Irish Churches, the Church of Ireland has given many of her sons and daughters to serve Christ far from the old country. But they have left imbued with that Irish Anglicanism that has more than once been referred to as "Anglicanism with a brogue"!

Herbert O'Driscoll was born in Connacht, not all that far from Knock he tells us. He was ordained priest in 1953 for the parish of Monkstown in Dublin. At present he is rector of Christ Church, Calgary, in Canada. His book, *Portrait of a Woman*, published in 1981, is probably the first extended marian devotional work by an Irish Anglican of which I am aware.

From the very beginning he makes clear to us that he is no theologian and that his work is devotional. Let me remind you, though, that behind his modesty lies the fact that he is one of the most respected Anglican priests in north America. In his time he has been Dean of Vancouver, Warden of the prestigious College of Preachers in Washington DC and is the author of numerous books on the art of preaching. Dr O'Driscoll is not just a simple country priest and this book bears the mark of the way in which he has been affected by a relationship with Mary the virgin. The meditations are in themselves a sort of life of Our Lady. The present age, strange and ambiguous in so many ways, is, he believes, somehow Mary's time.

> As one to whom the great shrine at Knock in the west of Ireland was familiar, I believe that there are those who have been vouchsafed visions of Mary, and that those visions have resulted in healing and holiness for unnumbered people.

And he adds:

> When the vast repository of beauty and terror which we call Christian tradition, the corporate memory of all Christians before me, tells me of Mary's virginity, of her immaculate conception, and of her assumption into heaven, I believe that truths have been preserved for me which, though I cannot fully explain them nor define them, I neglect to my loss.

Though with true Anglican caution he continues

> The question about whether these mysteries should or should not have been formed into dogmas is quite another and is one that need not concern us here.

In his final chapter, "The Roadway to the Stars", O'Driscoll writes.

> While Mary disappears from us as a woman of flesh and blood, living somewhere through the eventful first years of those growing communities, which would one day in far away Antioch be called Christian, she remains in the forefront of Christian history. Whatever be our particular stance toward a concept such as her bodily assumption into the heavenly realm, an unarguable fact remains: in the consciousness of Christians, Mary never died. . . the legend of the angels bearing Mary's tired and worn body to her Creator is a human attempt to express something impossible to explain yet equally impossible to deny. This "something" is the fact that, at least in some sense, Mary does not die, and that she has proved in countless lives to be a channel for the grace of her son.

And there we must leave it. I suppose one could say that Anglican mariology is that strange thing that always wants to say "Yes" except that it also wants immediately to add "but". This, I would say, simply reflects the four strands upon which all our theological method is built — scripture, tradition, reason and conscience. When all four can be satisfied then one's foundation is strong.

And mariology, that *relationship* with the virgin, not just thinking about her theologically, is probably more deeply implanted within our tradition today than at any other time in history. Small marian groups of Anglicans meet in Dublin and Belfast; pilgrimages to Walsingham from both cities have been a feature of recent years and have been led by parish clergy. On the ecumenical level Church of England bishops, priests and people have been invited to Lourdes and there have been given full liturgical facilities necessary for such a pilgrimage. Perhaps we may yet see a Church of Ireland party at Knock, officially invited and officially given liturgical facilities. Who knows?

Let me conclude with what is also the conclusion of O'Driscoll's book:

> We are passing where the road to Jericho crosses the Kidron valley. The upper church, built long ago by the Byzantines, has gone. In its place are the remains of the Crusader shrine. We move down steps which are long and wide. They begin in the blazing sun and deposit us in candlelit gloom, deep in the earth. Around us in this earth lies the dust of Crusader queens. A little further down we stand in the older walls of Byzantium, and then approach the tomb itself. Around it the crusaders placed a band of script.
>
> This is the Vale of Jeosaphat,
> where begins the roadway to the stars.
> Mary, favoured of God, was buried here,
> and incorruptible was raised to the skies.
> Hope of captives,
> their path, their light, their mother.

And O'Driscoll concludes:

> As we stand here, it should not shame us but rather give us all joy, that as we claim her son to be our brother, his life and death to be our Way, so we may claim this woman to be in God's providence and choosing "our path, our light, our mother".

6

MARY IN THE ORTHODOX
TRADITION*

Metropolitan Anthony

I will speak from the point of view of a believer, the way in which an Orthodox Christian perceives and venerates the mother of God. To begin with it might be wise to state that more often than not we use the expression "The mother of God". By this we do not obviously mean that the Blessed Virgin is the mother of God according to his Godhead but that she is the one who gave birth to the living God who became true man on earth. This is said only to avoid unnecessary confusion.

We venerate the mother of God above all creatures. To us she is the one whose perfect faith, whose perfect purity and whose great courage, both human and spiritual, made the Incarnation possible. We pray to her, according her with names that seem extravagant to certain people. We say about her that she is more "honourable than the Cherubim" and "infinitely more glorious than the Seraphim." Indeed she is the only creature of God in the world visible and invisible who has such oneness and such perfect unity with Christ her son, only begotten of the Father and only begotten of her. This is why we pray to her in a way in which we do not pray to saints. To saints we address our prayer asking them to pray for us. To the mother of God we exclaim "Save us" and again some find that this impinges on the rights of our only Saviour, Our Lord Jesus Christ. There are two reasons, I believe, why we address such a prayer to the mother of God. One is that of all creatures she is the one that is most perfectly at one with the will of God, not only in tune with, but at one with, the Divine will. In turning to her for prayers, for protection, we ask her to make real within our life the will of God.

It is as the mother of our Saviour that we turn to her, because she is at one with him but also — and this is something which has been impressing me deeply for a number of years as a result

*Text transcribed from tape was not edited by its author.

of experiences in both Soviet and communist dominated countries as well as elsewhere — if we think of her, if we realise that each of us by being a sinner not only in general terms but actual sin, that by continually choosing between God and the Adversary, between good and evil, between light and darkness in favour of all that is not of the Kingdom of God, that each of us by this active way in which we are sinners is truly directly responsible for the crucifixion, for the death of her only begotten son, and when we turn to her what we actually say in these words "Save us" is "Mother, I am the murderer of your son. If you forgive, if you become my advocate and protection, no one will be able to condemn me." And by doing this we see in her the incarnation, the expression of a love which is truly divine, which is truly the love of God the Saviour which has found its dwelling place in a human heart.

Faith
Now if we ask ourselves why we have this attitude to the mother of God then I think we can turn to the Gospel according to St Luke and remember the words which Elizabeth spoke to her when she came into her presence. "Blessed is she who has believed. It will be done to her according to your word." She is the one who from the beginning has been a vision to us of perfect trust in God, of believing him unreservedly and perfectly and in a way that was infinitely costly from the first moment to the last. We see on the day of the Annunciation the great Archangel proclaiming to her the coming of the Saviour through the Incarnation and the power of the Spirit in her of the only begotten son of God. It is interesting to compare the short dialogue between her and the Archangel with that which took place between Zechariah and him when he was promised a son who was later born as John the Forerunner. Zechariah has no doubt: "This cannot be.... My wife is too old.... Such things do not happen.... Give me a proof." And the proof that is given is that he is silenced. He is made mute. He cannot say one word of doubt until his doubt is resolved in the birth of John. The mother of God does not argue with the Archangel. She only says "How can that be? I am a virgin, I have known no man". And yet the conclusion of her question is an act of complete trust because when the Archangel tells her that the Holy Spirit of God will overshadow

her she accepts this without doubting, without hesitating. "I am the handmaid of the Lord. Let it be done to me according to your word".

Yet a thing which we forget about her is that the acceptance of this divine maternity was, from the point of view of her human situation, an immense risk. In Israel, a virgin, an unmarried woman giving birth to a child, was to be stoned. And what evidence could she give to people around her that it was a miraculous birth and not the result of an evil action. She accepts the danger and the risk of death because she leaves it to God to decide what he will do so that his will be fulfilled rightly according to his wisdom and love. Here she is truly the heir in the faith of the father of all believers, Abraham.

Abraham had also been put to a similar test. He too had been promised a son who would be the beginning of a vast race "as numerous as the stars of heaven, as the sand on the shore of the sea". Yet the same Lord commanded him to take this child and bring him a blood offering and Abraham did not oppose one promise of God to one command of God. He did not argue with God saying "But you are breaking your word. Have you changed your mind? How can this be? You promised me the life of this child and now you claim his death." He believed God more than he could believe his own understanding of the ways of God. Centuries before Isaiah had put it into words, he knew that the ways of God are as far above the ways of men as the thoughts of God are far above the thoughts of the sons of men.

Humility

The mother of God, also without demur, in a complete act of trust and humility accepts whatever may happen, provided it be God's own will fulfilled. I have used the word humility because in this particular context it is her true importance. The word humility comes from the Latin root "*humus*", meaning fertile ground. What is fertile ground? It lies fallow, silent, unresisting and helpless before the sky and the rest of creation. It receives with the same readiness and silently but completely the sunshine and the rain, receives equally the cutting furrow or the plough or the seed, accepts the refuse poured upon it, accepts everything and makes of everything a richness that will allow a richer and richer harvest to grow upon it. Humility is

97

total, contemplative silent generous surrender. It is a gift of self, a gift unreserved. And in a way it represents another aspect of the same mystery for the person which is expressed by virginity.

Virginity

Virginity is not a clinical condition. It is not the barren condition of a woman who has known no partner. It is the condition of one who has reserved his or her integrity in such a way, to such a perfection, that it is all given to the living Lord. It is so true what I have said about the difference between clinical and spiritual virginity that an eleventh-century writer said that tears of true repentance can give back to the person who has lost it even his physical virginity because God is the one who makes all things new. True repentance, that is, turning away radically, totally and perfectly from all evil, surrendering perfectly to the living God, being integrated into that mysterious body which is the body of Christ filled with the Spirit, can make one a new creature, not only a creature that behaves in a new way but is a new creature reborn by the Spirit of God.

She is the one who believes in perfect trust, in perfect humility, in perfect virginity of body and soul. We have, in the Orthodox Church, a feast which is not mentioned in the canonical gospels but in the so-called apocryphal gospels, the feast of the "Presentation of the mother of God to the temple". Historically it may have happened or one may well say that it did not happen. But what it conveys to us is much more important than whatever happened historically. The mother of God as a small child is brought and admitted to the Holy of Holies, that place into which the High Priest himself was allowed to enter only on rare occasions and after special purifications. She enters into the Holy of Holies which means that she enters into the heart of a communion with God. She enters into that relationship with God that will allow her to grow into the full measure of her human greatness, of her perfection. I will quote here not a theologian but an English writer Charles Williams, who sees Mary not only as the instrument of the Incarnation but as an active participant of the coming of the son of God into human history as a son of Mary. In one of his novels, *All Hallows Eve*, Williams describes in the following way the Incarnation. He says that when the time was right a maiden of Israel proved capable of pronouncing the holy name of God with all her mind, all her heart, all her will, all her flesh, and the Word became flesh. Obviously this is an image, but an image which carries a great deal of significance and truth. It is because she proved able to pronounce the name of God, and in Hebrew the name and person are co-extensive, that she was able to become the place of the Incarnation, the garden of Eden, "the holy place of God" as our liturgical books term her in places.

Cana

Then we enter into another passage of the gospel, this time John's, which pursues the same theme of she that had perfect faith. But now in the first place her faith in humility, in virginity, in perfect surrender, in true human holiness acquired through the struggle of a soul that emerged out of the twilight of the earth into the perfect light of God, is extended to and communicated to other people. Cana is a marriage feast of villagers, poor people. They had probably collected all their means and received the help of their friends to make the occasion as glorious as they could. But long before their hearts were satiated with joy, long before the guests were ready to go home of their own accord, wine failed them. The cans had probably run low, wine was no longer available. The feast was coming to an end, and yet everybody was still hungry and thirsty for the wonderful miracle which this wedding was. You will no doubt be aware of a passage from a manuscript of the gospel which is kept in one of the Cambridge libraries and has not become part of our canonical gospels. The Lord Jesus Christ we are told was asked by his disciples "When shall the Kingdom of God come?" And he answered "The Kingdom of God has already come when two are no longer two but one". This marriage feast was already the Kingdom of God come with power. It was indeed the beginning, an incipient Kingdom of God. But had not ancient writers such as Gregory of Nazianzen told us that marriage, established by God in paradise before the fall, is the only sacrament that survived the Fall and gained sacramental value, that is, a dimension of eternity and a measure of divinity to human love? Here we are drawn into the miracle of this Kingdom come with power.

They know that this kingdom must be conquered, that this is only the beginning, that bride and groom will have to take by force the kingdom and make it reality, day by day, hour by hour, but it is there in all its primeval beauty in order to practise all its tenderness and joy. It is hope blossoming out, it is love revealed. It is human joy acquiring the dimension of a divine event. And it must come to an end for God is gone, wine is no more.

But the mother of God calls to her divine son. She turns to him and says "They have no wine". There then follows a series of replies that seem so familiar to us that we no longer ask any questions about them. Yet it is so mightily illogical, so paradoxically contradictory that we should stop for a moment to think of it. The Lord answers his mother "What have I to do with thee? My hour has not yet come". A clear statement, if any statement can be clear. Yet it is prefaced by a question that may change the whole situation. St John Chrysostom says that this incident is typical of a mother who, having brought up her son to manhood, continues to think that she can continue to give him orders, to direct his life. The question the Lord is asking her is, "Why of all people, is it you that is turning to me? Why is it not the one presiding at the feast, or one of the relations, or even the bridegroom? Why is it you? Is it because you believe you are my mother according to the flesh and therefore have rights over me or...?" and he leaves the question open. The mother of God gives her answer but not, however, in words addressed to her divine son. She does not say, "But...". Rather, she turns to the servants and says to them "Whatsoever he may command you to do, do it". By saying these words she reveals that she believes in him as the son of God become the son of Mary, as the King of all, the Lord of all creation, the one who is the love of God incarnate, sacrificially offered unto death for the salvation of the world. Then the miracle occurs.

A moment ago Jesus had said "My hour has not yet come", the relationships were still human as it were, just mother and son. It was still the Old Testament. It was not yet the Kingdom, but when the mother proclaims her undivided faith and brings the servants into the mystery of her faith, then the Kingdom is established and Christ can act freely. This is in accordance with an old Jewish saying that God can enter any situation where a human person allows him to enter in. He does not force himself

either into a heart or into a life. As the image of the Book of
Revelation has it "I stand at the door and I knock". Yes he
stands at the door and he knocks. He waits. He does not force
his way except on the day when in order to save his disciples
from despair and defeat he entered through closed doors and
gave them his peace, that peace which the world cannot give
and gave them his Spirit, the Spirit of life eternal. Then a
second miracle occurs. We see how the faith of the mother of
God which was first total, heroic, sacrificial, extends now and
unfolds for other people making them partakers of her faith
and leaving to us, to all the world one unique command which
could resolve every human situation. Whatever Christ will
command you to do, do it. And we have his word in the gospel.

Presentation and Calvary
Now there is another aspect, a tragic aspect, to the person of
the mother of God. There are two events which I wish to bring
together because they do belong together, although they
appear at two ends of the gospel, Luke 2 and John 19. One is
the Presentation of our Lord in the temple and the other is the
Crucifixion. You will remember that every first-born male
child was to be brought to the temple as an offering to God.
What you may not perhaps remember as readily, is that this
rule was established by God in Exodus when he spoke to
Moses and said to him that, in exchange for the lives of the
first-born of Egypt that God doomed to death so that the
Israelites might be enabled to leave the land of their captivity,
the first-born of their own people must be brought to him, and
that he had right of life and death over them. It was to redeem
the blood of the first-born of Egypt that his children were to be
brought to him. And every mother who brought a child, a male
child, the first-born, the miracle of life for a woman, knew that
God had a right to say, "This one shall die". Centuries passed
and never did it happen, except once when the child brought to
the temple by the virgin mother was the only begotten son of
God, become the son of Mary. God did not end his life at that
moment. God allowed him to enter into manhood and into his
ministry. He allowed him to become the Saviour of the world,
not mechanically but by true participation of his humanity
with the will of God. At a certain moment he took him and
made of him the blood offering which every child might have

been. I know that I have said something which perhaps may not be clear enough to you because we have different backgrounds of thought.

In the Incarnation, the babe of Bethlehem is offered by God the Father to us in all his frailty. He is an image, an icon in Orthodox terms, of love divine. A love that is helpless, surrendered, given ultimately and totally vulnerable, offered to us, for us to take or reject, to use or to love. The child in Bethlehem is a vision of the frailty of love when it gives itself unreservedly. Speaking of St John the Baptist, the scripture tells us that he was given, and mankind could do with him what they wanted. They did. They killed the Forerunner and they crucified the Christ. But at that moment it is a one-sided act of God in which the human person of Christ is given passively. The person who is active is God within him, but not a newborn child. It is only when he has matured according to the flesh, and we see in St Luke's Gospel that he was growing in wisdom and in stature, it is when he has entered the full stature of his manhood, that he comes to the banks of the Jordan and enters his ministry. What some of us see in this event is this: John the Forerunner, the Baptist was preaching repentance, and hundreds and thousands came to the Jordan to be baptised. "Baptised" in Greek means to be merged completely into the waters. The immersion was on the limit perhaps of a sacramental act of grace by which these people were cleansed to the extent in which and the way in which they were truly repentant, turned away from evil, turned God-wards and became God's own people according to the wisdom of the Old Testament. Christ comes and John, seeing in him what Christ proclaimed later to his disciples at the Last Supper "the adversary is coming but there is nothing in me that belongs to him", seeing that the one who comes is pure of state, is in all ways perfect man except as far as sin is concerned, refuses, hesitates to baptise him. How can he wash the sins of him who is sinless? Christ commands him to do it. Christ merges into these waters of Jordan which have washed the sin, the evil, the godlessness of all sinners that came in repentance and emerges out of them carrying upon him the sin of mankind. A Protestant writer of France describing the event said to me "Isn't it like plunging white wool into dye? The wool is white and when it emerges it is purple with the dye that has clung to it". The same can be said about Christ. He enters free of death because he is at one with God, and humanity united with the Godhead cannot die. It is pervaded with eternal life. And he comes out clad with the purple of human sin and death.

We have an image of the same kind in human history. You will recall the story of Hercules and the Centaur. Hercules, the great Greek hero, wishing to free the country kills the Centaur, half-man half-beast, who was laying the country waste. The blood runs and the Centaur in order to avenge himself plunges his tunic into the blood and sends it to Hercules saying to him "Wear this tunic in memory of me". When Hercules puts on this tunic, however, it clings to his body, burning him apart. And he tears away this tunic from his flesh and dies. Is it not an apt image, in all its pagan imagery, of what happened to Christ? He merges into the sin of man and he dies of it, because it is not his death but our death that he dies.

Now to return to the Crucifixion. We all remember what happened. In Western art you see the cross with on one side the mother of God and on the other side, St John the Divine. More often than not the mother of God is fainting, crying in agony. In the gospel we see nothing of the sort, not that it did not happen, but it is not that side which the gospel meant to convey to us. Rather we see tragic silence, broken several times by the words of Christ, the silence of horror and the silence of communion. The mother of God at no moment turns to the soldiers who had crucified Christ, to the priests who are mocking him, to the curious people standing around. She does not say a word against the Crucifixion. As she brought the child to the temple on the day of the Presentation she fulfils her surrender of her child for the life and salvation of the world. She gives her child in total communion of wills with him, and with the Father who gave his only begotten son that the world might be saved. Here the act of faith as surrender, as humility, as gift, not only of what is ours but of what is us, comes to culminating point. Again indeed the point is well made in Luke 11 where, Jesus having spoken, one of the women present exclaims "Blessed are the breasts that fed thee. Blessed is the womb that carried thee". And the Lord says "More blessed are those who hear the word of God and fulfil it." She is the one who heard, who kept every word in her heart and fulfilled it by an ultimate and perfect sacrifice.

7

MARY AND WOMEN

Celine Mangan, OP

In Ireland today, and in the Catholic Church in general, it is possible to discern three types of relationship to Mary among women. Older women were brought up to look on Mary as a powerful protective mother and as an immaculate model of purity. With the emergence of a secularist society, and in the light of changing attitudes in the Church after Vatican II, the all-pervasive influence of Mary was largely lost so that very quickly a non-devotion to Mary became the practice for many women. Quite a number of women in Ireland today are at this stage, as I discovered when I questioned both older and younger women about their relationship with Mary. But others have rediscovered Mary as a woman among women and in this light see her as having much to offer to women of today.

A consideration of these three types of relationship might throw some light on the confusion that exists about Mary. There are those still in the first type of relationship who cannot understand why it has been left behind, while those who have changed can often feel guilty as a result. At the same time a more militant feminist attitude and the reactions to it have also to be considered.

"Bring flowers of the rarest . . ."
Studying the history of mariology down the centuries I have been struck by the fact that every age tends to make Mary into its own image and likeness, and it is often unfair for the next age to look askance at that which preceded it. Many of us today can look back with a certain nostalgia at May processions and Child of Mary ribbons and know that the caricature of these customs, such as appeared for instance in the television portrayal of Edna O'Brien's *Country Girls*, misses much of the point. And, yet, when we honestly ask ourselves what our attitude to Mary really was like then, we can find much that was bordering on superstition, for example the frantic praying

to Mary before examinations and promising to perform all kinds of feats in return for favours received.

As a protective mother, Mary was very real and still is to many women. She was there through the difficulties of life, especially of childbirth and in the rearing of children. The exaggeration of this protective role was to see Mary as the mother of mercy who would bring sinners by the back door into heaven in spite of the "justice" of God.

Mary as the immaculate model of purity was put forward as the ideal of young womanhood in our young days but an ideal which was modelled on the rather cold, anaemic statues of Mary which were prevalent at the time rather than on the real full-blooded woman of Nazareth. I would venture to suggest that this image of Mary owes more to a Victorian ideal of womanhood and to nineteenth century continental imports of devotion into Ireland than it does either to the real Mary or to the inheritance of our own native devotion to Mary. It seems to me from reading the literature that this was nearly always a warm, tender relationship, the essence of which was to stand *with* Mary looking towards her son:

> Come to me, loving Mary, that I may keen with you your very dear one.
> Alas, that your son should go to the cross, he who was a great diadem, a beautiful hero (from the Poems of Blathmac)[1]

The rosary is precisely this kind of a prayer when it is said properly and it was for this reason that it kept true faith alive in Ireland during times of persecution. In the early part of this century the Legion of Mary inherited the essence of this type of devotion to Mary which consists in looking towards God with Mary who shows us how to be active in his service.

Traditional Irish devotion to Mary, then, was firmly rooted at the heart of true Christian devotion but in the thirties and forties in Ireland there was a tendency to set Mary apart and to give her more and more honour. It was felt that one could never honour her enough and that her son would not want to honour his mother less. Hymns like "Bring Flowers of the Rarest" bring us back to such a time.

Part of the reason for this exaggeration was undoubtedly sectarian. Because Protestants did not seem to honour Mary enough, Catholics went to the other extreme. The unfortunate result of this has been that, while Protestants in England and the continent are rediscovering Mary as part of their heritage, many in Ireland, especially among Northern Presbyterians, totally reject her still. One clergyman told me that he was nearly run out of his church for preaching a sermon on the Magnificat — and the Magnificat is straight out of the Bible which Protestants have always held so dear.

Some time ago the Catholic bishops and the Irish Council of Churches set up a sub-committee of which I was a member. We hammered out a common statement of beliefs which stressed Mary's relationship to her son as mother and which saw her as part of the nucleus of the emergent Church in Jerusalem. She is to be seen as "worthy of imitation for her faith, her prayer and pondering, her ready response and steadfast following of her son." We will come back again to the essence of this statement.

Mary and feminism
During the meetings of that sub-committee, it struck me over and over again that the other members of that study group, because they were all male — formed by a clerical theological training whether Protestant or Catholic — were far closer to one another at one level than to me as the only woman present. And here we all were solemnly discussing a woman! What could we hope to say to ordinary women? I think my interest in the feminist questioning of the traditional understanding of Mary dates from those meetings.

Dear as the traditional picture of Mary still is to many of us, I think we must be willing to face the questioning of that picture by the insights of our own generation which include those of feminists. In every age the Church has had to face the challenge of new ways of putting things; it is not the faith in itself which changes but the language, culture and thought patterns in which it is expressed.

There are many things in the traditional picture of Mary with which some women feel unhappy today. When countering feminist arguments about the low place accorded to women in the Church, it is not enough to say that women, rather, have a high place in the Catholic Church because of the great honour in which Our Lady is held. This is precisely the problem: woman in Mary, on the one hand, has been exalted to the heights while on the other she is seen as the temptress and, therefore, as impure. In ordinary life women are neither at one end or the other of these extremes and sometimes one feels that it is because a patriarchal Church cannot cope with real women in the flesh that it relegates women to these abstract extremes. As Rosemary Reuther, one of the best-known women theologians in the United States, puts it:

> Official mariology validates the twin obsessions of male fantasies towards women; the urge to both reduce the female to the perfect vehicle of male demands, the instrument of male ascent, and at the same time to repudiate the female as the source of all that pulls him down into bodiliness, sin and death. Mariology exalts the virginal, obedient, spiritual feminine and fears all real women in the flesh.[2]

While one may like to question that last sentence of hers, it is perhaps indicative that it is I, as a woman religious, who was asked to speak on Mary and women at this conference rather than a married woman. (At least it is better than having a man speak on the subject which is what would have happened a very short time ago.) In many ways in the Church in Ireland it is only sisters who have been allowed the independence to develop themselves as women. Other women by and large have been too preoccupied with pleasing the male society in which they live whether as wives, mothers, consumers, or obedient church goers.

It is because Mary has been made the epitome of male ambivalence towards women that she has been neglected and even rejected by many feminists at the present time:

> The more remote and unreal the personal feminine is, the more intense is the male's yearning for a projection of an "eternal feminine".[3]

Putting Mary on a pedestal as the "eternal feminine" has excused men, especially clerics, from having to face the reality of women. Of course women are as much to blame for this as men because we have gone along in the complicity and have been content with things the way they are. Men are as much the losers as women by the fact that half the gifts of the human race are not used to the full. I remember once suggesting to a bishop an area of improvement in parish structures. He told me that I was the third *woman* who had made such a suggestion to him. Women's particular insights have much to offer the Church and the world.

Feminists reject totally the picture of Mary as the "eternal feminine" but, at the same time, there are many aspects of mariology with which at least some do relate. Because God has been cast in an almost exclusively male role in the Judaeo-Christian religion, as Father, Creator, Power, there is at least the feeling that Mary has preserved something of the feminine near to the Godhead. It is quite clear from the history of the Church that Mary took over many of the characteristics of the goddesses of pagan religions. I remember coming across a beautiful Madonna once in an archeological site in Israel and being a bit nonplussed to discover that it was a portrait of the goddess Isis and her son Horus rather than that of Mary and Jesus. By confining the feminine goddess images to Mary the Church has been left free to see God only in male terms.

Of course God is neither male nor female but we have only human language in which to speak of the divine and that language is shot through with sexual bias. If God can be considered as Father why not as Mother? Indeed there are many passages in the Bible where the mother image is used for God; even when spoken of as father many of the characteristics mentioned are those which we would attribute to a mother. Hosea 11: 1-4 is a good example:

When Israel was a child I loved him,
out of Egypt I called my son . . .
Yet it was I who taught Ephraim to walk,
who took them in my arms;
I drew them with human cords,
with bands of love;
I fostered them like one
who raises an infant to his cheeks;
Yet, though I stooped to feed my child,
they did not know that I was their healer.

In a recent encyclical, Pope John Paul draws attention to the fact that the characteristics of God's compassion and forgiveness in the Bible are actually feminine qualities; indeed the word for mercy in Hebrew is actually taken from the word for the womb:

> From the deep and original bond — indeed the unity —
> that links a mother to her child there springs a particular
> love. Of this love one can say that it is completely
> gratuitous, not merited and that in this aspect it con-
> stitutes an interior necessity, an exigency of the heart . . .
> The word for mercy generates a whole range of feelings;
> including goodness and tenderness, patience and under-
> standing, that is readiness to forgive.[4]

I think that all of us in the Church, men and women alike,
should consciously relate to these more feminine ways of
speaking of God because in so doing we will have a much
richer insight into the divinity. It is not enough to pay lip
service to what is there in the Bible; we have to bring its insights
right into our prayer and our lives. This will allow Mary free to
be a woman among women again and therefore to have much
to say to women today precisely as real women.

Mary: a woman among women
The way forward for a true relationship between Mary and
women would therefore seem to be not so much to see her in
splendid isolation as the symbol of the "eternal feminine", but
firmly established among the women disciples of her son.[5]
Disentangling the characteristics of these other women in the
gospels has helped me to understand Mary of Nazareth a little
better.

As the early Church looked back to the time of Jesus the
many Marys with whom he was associated tended to get
confused especially as a male dominated Church increasingly
relegated women to an inferior position. The other Marys were
conflated into the traditional portrait of Mary Magdalene who
emerged as the sinful woman par excellence and, therefore, as
the antithesis of Our Lady. But nowhere in the gospels is Mary
Magdalene regarded as a sinful woman. In Luke 8: 1-3 she is
listed among the women followers of Jesus. There it is said of
her that "seven devils" were driven out of her. But elsewhere in
the gospels, the driving out of evil spirits relates to deliverance
from illness. The reason they were presumed to be sexual devils
here was because of the tendency in the tradition to link Luke 8
with the story which precedes it in Luke 7: that of the *unnamed*

sinful woman who anointed the feet of Jesus. Mary was probably healed from a physical or psychological disorder, therefore, and so ever afterwards her faith would be based on the nearness of the one who had cured her.[6] She would follow him, minister to him right up to the cross and beyond. John's account of their meeting after the Resurrection is worth looking at again:

> Jesus said to her, "Mary!" She turned to him and said, "Rabbuni" (meaning "Teacher"). Jesus then said: "Do not cling to me, for I have not yet ascended to the Father. Rather, go to my brothers and tell them, I am ascending to my Father and your Father, to my God and your God!"
>
> *(Jn 20: 16-17)*

What is meant here by Jesus' saying to her: "Do not cling to me"? In an older interpretation of Mary Magdalene's story, this was very often linked with the patriarchal idea of the impurity of women: Jesus was holy and could therefore not be touched by a woman. Modern understanding of feminine psychology has given us a deeper insight into this passage. What is probably involved is Jesus telling Mary that the former way of relating to him is over; her faith must mature and not depend on the visible nearness of the one who has meant everything to her. She must let go in order to find him at a deeper level. Mary learnt the lesson and so became the first apostle, sent by Jesus to tell the other apostles that he was risen. Mary Magdalene's lesson of letting go is one most women have to learn; we all have experience of the clinging female or the possessive mother. Women need to let go of their dependence and discover the power within themselves to be full persons in their own right.

Mary of Nazareth had that ability to let go. As she appears in the Infancy narrative in particular, she is someone who was wide open to a totally new way of relating to God and to the world other than what she had been accustomed to up until then. The scriptures do not give us a picture of a willowy, fainting female such as many of the artists' impressions of the Annunciation portray, but of a clear-headed and strong-minded young woman who was ready to fly in the face of the accepted norms and customs of her time. Her "Let it be done to me" was not the kind of resigned putting up with the will of God with which we in Ireland are all too familiar. It was, instead, a positive reaching out towards God's new way of acting, towards understanding his good pleasure (which is what the word "will" really means in the Bible) that his people would be saved.

Mary's saying of "Let it be done to me" did not make everything clear at once for her, so Luke's favourite word for discipleship is "pondering". Another Mary is Luke's symbol for this pondering:

> On their journey Jesus entered a village where a woman named Martha welcomed him to her home; she had a sister named Mary, who seated herself at the Lord's feet and listened to his words. Martha who was busy with all the details of hospitality, came to him and said, "Lord are you not concerned that my sister has left me to do the household tasks all alone? Tell her to help me." The Lord in reply said to her: "Martha, Martha, you are anxious and upset about many things; one thing only is required. Mary has chosen the better portion and she shall not be deprived of it."
>
> *(Lk 10: 38-42)*

This Mary was Jesus' friend from the house in Bethany (we will come back to Martha) and the gospel portrait of her here shows her in the true attitude of a disciple: in training at the Rabbi's feet as Paul was, for instance, at the feet of Gamaliel (Acts 22:3). Probably in real life Mary was one of the few people, men or women, who really listened to Jesus, listened to him as he worked through the implications of his mission. She would have acted as a sounding board for his ideas — and his fears. She had the privilege of listening to the Word of the Lord himself but we have all got to search the Scriptures and see that word open up before us for our time so that our hearts will "burn inside us" at the sound of it *(Lk 24:32)*.

Luke shows Our Lady as having that same attitude of pondering the word (see Lk 2: 19, 51). The word, "ponder", means to throw together and interpret dark and difficult things and Mary's pondering of the Scriptures must have put before her the dark and difficult ways her son would have to follow. But hearing and pondering the word is not enough; one has to act upon it. The woman in the crowd around Jesus said: "Blest is the womb that bore you and the breasts that nursed you," but Jesus replied: "Rather, blest are they who hear the word of God and keep it" (*Lk 11: 27-28*).

Many have interpreted this passage as downgrading Mary but what Luke is pointing out is that it is not physical relationship to Jesus which counts but following him as a disciple (see 8: 19-21). How, then, did Mary "keep" the word? A look at another woman in the gospels might help us to probe a bit deeper here.

Martha gets a bad press in Luke 10. In fact, although down through the centuries a parallel was drawn between Mary and Martha as being the symbols of the contemplative and the active life, in this passage Martha is not a disciple at all. But in another passage (Jn 11: 17-28) Martha is the one who acts as a disciple while Mary sits at home and mopes. This is an interesting example of human psychology: Mary's strong point in quiet attentiveness becomes her weakness in the face of crisis, while what had been Martha's weak point in everyday life now becomes her strength. She shows herself as decisive, ready to question and argue with Jesus, asserting her need and ready to fight for it. In so doing, she reaches a pinnacle of faith in Jesus which few others in the New Testament come to when she says: "I have come to believe that you are the Messiah, the Son of God, he who is to come into the world" (*Jn 11:27*). In the synoptics the primacy of faith belongs to Peter (see Mt 16:16) while in John it comes from a woman.[7]

The picture of Our Lady in the gospels has much of this decisiveness of Martha: there was no mooning around or dithering after the message of the angel. She was ready to argue until she was clear what to do; then she became the practical woman of action, ready to help her old cousin in her need. She is shown as making the most of a difficult situation in the stable; not bemoaning her fate but making use of whatever was to hand. She is, then, a real model for women today, where firm, decisive action is needed to find the true place of women in the Church and in society at large.

The prayer of Mary, the Magnificat, shows her as this kind of firm, decisive person. The use of the Magnificat can often be a barometer of how Mary is considered in any particular age. Earlier paraphrases tended to stress the interiority of Mary and her relationship with God, with barely a sidelong glance at the issues of the poor and of justice which it raises, while many present-day translations put all the stress on such issues. Last year I had to talk on a panel about Mary on Radio Ulster's *Sunday Sequence*. One of the people who phoned in was a woman from Derry. She spoke very movingly of the image she had come to of Mary which was largely based on such a present-day understanding of the Magnificat. She saw Mary as someone who was aware of the sufferings of her time and even belligerent about what needed to be done. As the woman from Derry talked on I was somewhat aggrieved as she was using up one of my main points. But, as I shifted the Magnificat card to the bottom of my pile of aides mémoire, I felt very excited too — excited that women in Ireland were getting behind the stereotype into which Mary had been cast and could look afresh at what the Scriptures had to say about her.

One final look at the other Marys in the gospel. There was Mary, the wife of Clopas (Jn 19:25), another Mary (Mt 27:61), Mary, mother of James (Mk 15:40). Whether these are one person or several can be debated but, one or many, they form part of the group which followed Jesus to the cross when the male disciples had nearly all fled. Maybe "hanging in there", to use the popular expression, is one of the greatest gifts of women. Suffering with the Lord is part and parcel of discipleship and both John and Luke show Mary as sharing in that suffering: Luke by the prophecy of Simeon (Lk 2:25) and John by placing her standing at the foot of the cross (Jn 19:25). Today's women disciples are no strangers to the kind of obedience to the Word which can lead to suffering and death. People like Jean Donovan in El Salvador and our own Sr Joan Sawyer from Belfast who was killed recently in South America bear this out.

Summary
The most important document on Mary to emerge from the Holy See in recent years was Pope Paul VI's *Guidelines for Marian Devotion*. In it he emphasised that devotion to Mary today should be "scriptural, liturgical, ecumenical and anthropological." The relationship to Mary which I have been outlining fulfils all four of these criteria. It is solidly based on the picture of Mary which emerges from the Scriptures and the

liturgy. From the ecumenical point of view it fulfils the findings of the inter-faith committee which I mentioned earlier that Mary be seen as "worthy of imitation for her faith, her prayer and pondering, her ready response and steadfast following of her son". Finally, by seeing Mary as a woman among women, it gives her back again her full humanity.

We must no longer regard Mary, then, as an abstract entity to be idolised or rejected, but as a very full woman who can help us to live our Christianity as truly liberated women. Such liberation must lead us, however, to a deeper commitment to the liberation of others, both of men and of women.

8

THE IMPACT OF FEMINISM
ON MARIOLOGY

Donal Flanagan

For some the idea that feminism has any role in regard to mariology may seem strange, bizarre, even perverse. Feminism is a modern philosophical anthropology which presents a view of humankind seen from the perspective of women. It is in some of its forms anti-male, sometimes even anti-Christian, and at times indeed specifically anti-marian. It seems *a priori* unlikely it can have anything to offer towards a more coherent and contemporary mariology. Mariology, for its part, is an attempt to present the theological truths of Christian revelation about Mary as a whole. It is the systematic presentation of one woman's role in the Christian salvation. It has historically served to present Christians with Mary as a model of the Christian woman.

Feminist writers take different approaches to mariology. For some, marian doctrine is token feminism at the heart of a fundamentally patriarchal, anti-feminist religion, Christianity. For such feminists mariology is the doctrine of the tamed feminine, the doctrine which affirms as much about the creativity and power of woman as a male-dominated patriarchal religion can allow itself. For such feminists marian doctrine is as irrelevant as the patriarchal religion which is its matrix.

Not all feminists however take this extreme line. For some, mariology as it has evolved historically is problematic but not necessarily anti-feminist in its essence. These writers take issue with the historical shape of marian doctrine, seeing this as distorted. They attribute this distortion to the male's ambivalence about women and ultimately about his own femininity.

Feminists point out that mariology historically has presented Christians with an implied "high" doctrine of woman — it might be described as the doctrine of the ideal woman. The doctrine of woman implied in mariology, however, is only part of the Christian doctrine of woman. Christianity in addition to its high doctrine about woman implied in mariology, also has an explicit "low" doctrine about woman which occurs in differing formulations but seems to cluster particularly round the notion of woman as Eve. Feminists point out further that the doctrine of woman implied in Mary and the more explicit doctrine of woman related to the concept of Eve are very firmly linked historically. While mariology is not *directly* responsible for the low doctrine of woman current in Christianity from early times, it helps to keep this doctrine there by its opposing linkage to it, through the Eve doctrine.

The shaping of the marian tradition can be traced historically. The figure of Mary assimilated current feminine images. For example, in the East the virgin of the gospels came gradually over time to be presented as the lady of Power, the Empress. In the Western Church by contrast Mary of Nazareth appeared to fourth century ascetics above all as the virgin, the model of their lives dedicated to Christ. This occurred under the influence of Ambrose writing for the women under his guidance. Again, in the world of medieval chivalry Mary was presented as *Notre Dame* — the Woman of Inspiration, the Ideal Woman of chivalry. It is plain, particularly from the last example quoted, that the historical shaping of mariology took place in a male-conditioned mould, in a male-oriented thought-world. The figure of Mary in the tradition took on certain symbolic accretions. She came to express the male ideal of what woman should be.

It is not surprising that if, for those feminists who try to come to grips with marian doctrine (as opposed to those who reject it outright), the doctrines about Mary appear as doctrines which indirectly or directly affirm the idea of woman's inferiority to man and underpin this idea. The ideal woman is passive, indecisive — the opposite of all those qualities which the male values in himself. The success of this image of Mary in the tradition is one more evidence of the power of the framework over the biblical data. Mariology can thus appear to feminists as a doctrine which exists in the vacuum created by the denigration of woman endemic to Christianity from the beginning and which feeds off this denigration and actually reinforces it. Mary needs Eve.

Feminist critique and Reformation critique

The Reformation can from one very particular standpoint be

viewed as a critique of medieval mariology, although Mary was not among the major formal issues in dispute. The theological stripping which Luther and others attempted (see Luther on the Magnificat) was dedicated to a humanisation of Mary, an attempt as Luther saw it to let the image of the Maid of Nazareth emerge from the gold trappings of the medieval Queen of Heaven.

The feminist critique or more accurately the critique implied in feminist writing about Mary is addressed impartially to Catholic, Reformation and Orthodox thinking. It is a critique with a truly ecumenical drive for it finds all the traditions blameworthy or at the very least not conscious enough of the male mould in which their theological understanding of Mary has been forged.

A move towards feminist concerns: *Marialis cultus,* 34-37
Already in 1974, that most modern-minded man, Pope Paul VI was expressing clearly the need for mariology to grow through some kind of process of sifting away its historically conditioning elements into a doctrine to which a twentieth-century woman could relate. While the points he made may appear to some marginal, they do offer an invitation to theologians to move forward along the road of attending to the demands and preoccupations of twentieth-century women so as to present a Virgin Mary current to this age, a recognisable woman of our time. This invitation of the Pope made to a mariology in shock, if not in decline, has not really been taken up and has certainly not emerged as the wave of the future. It seems to me that mariology will limp along until it faces up to this challenge squarely.

Conclusion
The theologian facing feminist critiques of Mary and marian doctrine both implied and expressed can dismiss them as irrelevant to his inherited understanding of Mary which he sees as basically determined by biblical and traditional data. This fundamentalist stance is, however, hardly a real option, if theology is to continue as a serious intellectual inhabitant of the twentieth century.

At the opposite pole the marian theologian can go a

different road and try to learn something from the extreme feminist critique of Christianity as patriarchal. Refusing to accept its conclusions that historical Christianity is irredeemably patriarchal and that its marian doctrine is necessarily vitiated by this fact, he can begin the long laborious process of raising the questions of how far we can rid Christianity of its exclusivist male symbolism for God and the divine and what consequences this must have for marian doctrine as it is currently shaped. These questions can only be raised here; any attempt to answer them would stretch far beyond this short communication.

Of more immediate possibility, without entering those depths, would be an attempt to respond to the demands of reformist feminism. The figure of Mary must no longer be employed as a symbol to divide women (Eve/Mary) or to subordinate women to men. The Eve/Mary comparison must be recognised as the product of male thinking and must be simply left on one side, as its correction seems inherently impossible. As a practical expression of this change it might not be out of order to propose some public admission of its necessity. Since Vatican II the Roman Catholic Church has found the spiritual strength to ask forgiveness of the Jewish people, and the present Pope has presided over reassessments of the Church's stance in regard to Luther and Galileo. But not a word about women — only the barren assertion that they cannot be priests.

It is long past the time for a public statement from the Churches admitting the damage the schizoid theology of Eve and Mary has caused and owning up to the fact that there is a link between this kind of thinking at the theological level and the way women are regarded generally in the Church.

It is partly this low theological view of women, but even more the over-emphasis on the theological significance of the maleness of Jesus that has got the Roman Catholic Church into the impasse in which it rests on the ordination of women. Progress here is contingent on the admission of the fact that the maleness of Jesus is not of theological significance, that the marian symbol needs to be correspondingly defeminised, (its femaleness is not theologically significant) and the theology of woman needs to be upgraded to the study of a symbol which is fully fit to express, and capable of expressing, the divine.

Questions from feminists about Mary are questions to all the Churches and to each one of us.

9

MARY AND YOUTH TODAY

Patricia Coyle

About a year ago an older colleague of mine at UCD was talking about his student days at that institution. He remarked that in his time, it would only be the really courageous person who would have the gumption not to stand up and say the Angelus when the bell rang in the library. Nowadays, he said, the situation would be reversed, and it would certainly take courage of the highest order to stand up alone and pray in the library at the Angelus hour!

I remember distinctly my youthful amazement at how much things had changed in twenty-five years and I'm sure that many people have been witnesses, beneficiaries and victims of many changes —religious and secular — in those same years. Certainly we all have witnessed one of the most powerful movements of renewal in the Church —the Second Vatican Council. But while the very few would deny the greatness of the Spirit-filled vision of that Council, it may well be said that it was much better on "ideas" than on their actual implementation. This fact coupled with the fast accelerating forces of secularisation in the modern world, leaves 1989 looking very different from 1964. There is a marked decrease in certain numbers attending church and liturgy; a marked increase in atheism and religious indifference, and a general distaste or distrust of devotional piety in many quarters, especially among the young.

It is not surprising that within this milieu the whole question of Mary has for many young people, become boring at least, at worst irrelevant. The devotional practices so familiar to our older generation which reached their zenith with Pope Pius XII's proclamation of the dogma of the Assumption followed by the Marian Year of 1954, are no longer meaningful or accessible to the vast majority of our youth today.

Perhaps the picture looks very bleak? Frankly I don't think so. I firmly believe that we are living in a time of great potential for a renewed understanding of the heart of our Christianity. G.K. Chesterton once said that true Christianity has never been tried and I think he is right. A fullness of understanding regarding Christianity also necessitates a deeper awareness of the role of Mary, mother of Christ, model of the Church.

Symbols and our times
The philosopher Eric Voegelin analyses three stages in the process of humankind's experience of transcendent reality or God[1].

1. The subject's experience of objective transcendence — God.

2. The experience becomes articulated and thereby more fully understood, by being expressed in verbal concepts, symbols, ritual or gesture. Over the years these articulations may solidify and become familiarised (even distorted) and eventually breaking off from the original engendering experience, we may have devotion and ritual practice *for the sake of practice and devotion* rather than because of any true understanding or re-evoking of original experience. Even the language used in connection with the original experience may become mystifying or naively simplistic.

3. Finally the third stage is the rejection of the symbols, liturgy, words, dogma, devotion, by a generation that has found them meaningless and who are totally cut off from the engendering original experience. Today I believe we youth are in grave danger of throwing out many such symbols/ devotion, rituals/liturgies, because they have become meaning- less to us. Attempts have been made to supply us with artificially "meaningful" symbols and "theologies" as we indulge in frenetic searches for new meanings. I feel this is only wallpapering. The real task is for us all to get in touch with the truth of the original experiences that gave rise to the rich symbolic-theological-liturgical heritage that is ours, so that we can build on them from our own experience. This is particularly true in relation to our understanding of Mary, who as a religious figure has suffered more than most from inaccurate portrayal, distortion and dangerously false "theologies". So how are we to regain a true and living awareness of Mary in

121

order that we may understand our Christianity more fully? Theologian, mariologist and colleague, Fr Chris O'Donnell, warns us that "the mere recitation of marian prayers will not be enough to renew and deepen devotion to Mary or to draw our non-Roman brothers to appreciate the riches we have in the Church".[2]

Eric Voegelin makes a call for a "meditative reconstitution" of the original spiritual experiences — Paul Ricoeur calls it de-mythologising in order to re-mythologise.

Briefly stated they ask that we open ourselves to mystery; that we be prepared to entertain that which we do not fully understand. A meditative reconstitution requires that we take time to get in touch with our own experience of self and others, cultivating the eye of faith that can see God's hand at work in us and in the world. It requires that we open ourselves to the scholarly insights and wisdom of those who spend their time in genuine pursuit of truth, from a standpoint of openness and humility. In short it requires something like what has been happening here all week: prayers; wisdom; reflection; intellectual understanding. There is a meditative reconstitution taking place here this week which will, I believe, dispose us to not just a devotional knowledge of Mary but a knowledge of the heart of that great woman.

And indeed since Vatican II and in particular since the mid-1970s there has been a deepening awareness on the part of theologians and scholars and laity (e.g. Charismatic Renewal, Teams of Our Lady) concerning the question of Mary and the Church. In particular we think of the very fine document by Paul VI, *Marialis cultus.* I would like to share briefly with you what I believe to be basic fruits of this renewed work of the Spirit in mariology and the potential power of this ever deepening understanding of Mary to speak to all of us but particularly to the young who face so many challenges in this very complex modern world of ours.

Perhaps one of the most powerful and fallacious expectations which has been cultivated in the youth of today is what I call "the expectation of omniscience". From many sources, we young are encouraged to believe that reality can be fully encompassed by our knowing of it. We are encouraged to "think rationally," look for proof (always of a scientific nature — but of course we are kept in the dark about the real nature of scientific proof — more accurately called scientific *disproof!*) The truth of any fact is guaranteed because we "saw it on TV", read it in a newspaper that "tells it all" and "reveals the inside story". We are trained in more and more sophisticated ways of knowing in order that we might never be ignorant; in order that reality can be "got at" by us. Our relationship with the complexity of reality has been reduced to that of power and management — we understand it so we control it — mini-Frankensteins in a world where knowledge is synonymous with power, and mystery synonymous with weakness or superstition. Our quest for omniscience is of course doomed. Evil abounds as does violence, destruction, natural disasters, injustices, and always the events which we do not understand. We are left bewildered, asking "Why?" or we flee to surrogate cults and sects in an effort to attain enlightenment, or we try to alleviate our boredom and sense of meaningless despair through drugs or alcohol.

The philosopher Gabriel Marcel says that we in the modern world have lost touch with the very heart of reality. We seek to destroy the very essence of life by dissecting it in order to understand. We have, he claims, lost the ability to "wait on reality," to receive it with "ontological humility"; to be disposed from the depths of our being to the fact that the truth always transcends our knowing of it — that we do not possess the truth but that somehow truth may possess us; and that mystery is a vital part and parcel of life. We have therefore lost faith in the ultimate goodness of life. We can no longer say a cosmic "Yes" like the people of Newgrange — our ancestors, who built a burial chamber through which the sun would penetrate into its darkest recesses on the shortest day of the year, the mid-Winter solstice. Neither can we say a religious "Yes" like the holy Julian of Norwich who proclaimed "And all will be well. . . and all will be well: and all manner of things will be well."

Mary, model for our world
The antidote to our distorted relationship with reality, and the greatest model of anthropological humility, and the person whose life says more than any philosopher ever could, is of course, Mary. Every encounter we have with her in the gospels reveals to us a woman whose "Yes" to God was total, from the

123

depths of her being, while her actual comprehension of exactly what was happening was far from perfect. We think of the Annunciation and Mary asking "How can this be?", only to follow her questions with complete acceptance of God's desire for her. She wondered when the shepherds came to visit at Bethlehem; she was puzzled by the painful words of Simeon the prophet and she did not understand when Jesus apparently got lost and was found teaching in the temple. Luke 2:51 sums it up for us: "She pondered all these things in her heart." Certainly Mary never had all the answers, least of all at Calvary, but she was there with the apostles — as a woman of faith — in the upper room at Pentecost.

Furthermore, Mary's faith and truth was not just a passive, stoic acceptance of life and what was being doled out to her. No, her fiat was an *active receptivity* of the grace of God. We know from the Greek, that her response of "Let it be done unto me according to thy word" was really a *joyful* and *enthusiastic* reply. This joyful embracing of reality in the belief that "all things will work to good for those who love God" is also evidenced in that beautiful hymn of praise, the Magnificat, recorded by Luke. The ultimate goodness of God is such that

> He who is mighty has done great
> things for me,
> Holy is his name
> And his mercy is from generation
> unto generation for those who fear him.

At Cana when Jesus said that his time had not yet come, Mary displayed the same knowing trust, turning to the steward and simply saying "Do whatever he tells you".

Now more than ever we young need to believe in Mary as model of joyful humility, who helps us toward discovering a reality greater than ourselves, ultimately good, conferring on us a special status as beloved of God, wherein we find our own blessedness and may sing our own Magnificat. Paul VI tells us in *Marialis cultus* that we as a Church can act like Mary especially in liturgy when "with faith we listen, accept, proclaim and venerate the Word of God: distribute it to the faithful as the bread of life, and in the light of that word examine the signs of the times and interpret and live the events of history."[3]

It must be acknowledged that as we do examine the signs of the times, and interpret and live the events of history, we are faced with an enormous record of pain and suffering and especially in our generation of potential global annihilation; there is therefore in the twentieth century a great tendency toward fatalism, absurdity and despair. Mary, once again in this light serves as a powerful incarnational witness of the true profoundly Christian virtue of *hope*. She is a profound symbol for us of the healing of body and soul in the midst of an all too broken world. This discovery of Mary as living symbol of healing came for me, from two of the most unlikely places — it came from the marian dogmas which used to mean very little to me at all.

The Immaculate Conception
My own somewhat naive and childish understanding of this dogma was to believe that life was easy for Mary; she was perfect, but the rest of us would have to struggle with temptation not being preserved as she was, from original sin. Now it is clear that the dogma of the Immaculate Conception is really a proclamation of good news for us. Mary was preserved from original sin by dint of the fact that Jesus too *would die for her*. As such she is the recipient of a tremendous grace and as the Vatican II document on liturgy puts it, she is "the most excellent fruit of redemption".[4] She is preserved from actual and original sin by the loving kindness of God in his redeeming son, and thus she becomes a profound sign of hope for us since she is God's chosen witness that we too can be recipients of this healing mercy. This is no mere wishful thinking for surely this is the message Jesus tries to convey so forcefully in the passage from Mark 3:32-35.

> A crowd was sitting round him at the time the message was passed to him, "Your mother and brothers and sisters are outside asking for you". He replied, "Who are my mother and my brothers?" And looking round at those sitting in a circle about him, he said, "Here are my mother and my brothers. Anyone who does the will of God, that person is my brother and sister and mother."

And again in Luke 11:27-29:

> Now as he was speaking a woman in the crowd raised her

voice and said, "Happy the womb that bore you and the breasts you sucked!" But he replied, "Still happier those who hear the word of God and keep it!"

Likewise the dogma of the Assumption (which could be viewed as merely a nice gesture to honour Mary) can be seen also to have far-reaching implications. In that dogma Mary, as one of us is firmly guaranteed the status of heaven — one of the redeemed. She is the model of fully healed and restored humanity in a world where we can be all too tempted to doubt the basic goodness of humankind at all. She is the symbol of the glorious life — the reality — to which we are all called not next year, or on our own deathbed, but *here* and *now*. In the face of the evil, negativity, despair and neurosis of our modern world, Mary in her Assumption is once again the symbolic "Yes" — the symbolic witness to Christ's claim that death is conquered, evil can be and is overcome, that the victory is ours. Mary is the "new Eve" in the Patristic tradition: "Death through Eve, life through Mary." Through her Immaculate Conception and Assumption Mary witnesses to the fact that God's healing salvific grace is for everyone. It is fitting that the place where she declared "I am the Immaculate Conception" (Lourdes) is also the biggest shrine of healing in the world.

Yet another way in which Mary stands as foil to the pressures of today's world on the young is in her counter-witness to what I call the fallacious assumption of fulfilment. There has been a trend in the last ten years or so which briefly stated assumes that the purpose of life is to be fulfilled. It finds expression in many ways and in our vastly consumerist society it comes in the form of overt encouragement to buy as much as we can in order to make sure we are happy. At a psychological level it can be expressed in what I call the "*Kramer vs Kramer* syndrome." I refer to the film in which a woman leaves her husband and young child for no other reason than "to find herself." In this way self-fulfilment is insidiously portrayed as something that comes from some mythical place "without" but certainly never from the capacities within ourselves. It is a pervasive ideology which has become an unspoken drive for many of our young people. It leads to a grasping mentality, a desire for success, recognition and approval from others at all costs — in short it is a wordly wisdom. It is not however, I would argue, the wisdom of Christianity. The whole life of

Christ was one of *self-emptying*, self-giving. It was a life which spent itself for others in endless living, giving and healing. As Paul tells us in Philippians 2: 6-7, "Though he was of God, Jesus did not consider equality with God a thing to be grasped: emptying himself he took the form of a slave." And as theologian Rosemary Reuther has pointed out, the revolutionary quality of Jesus was his insistence upon the overthrowing of power relationships so that the greatest among the disciples was to become the servant.[5] Self-fulfilment, if it makes any sense in Christian terms, means its opposite: it means self-emptying, we must die to ourselves.

Mary, surely, is a perfect model of this process of active self-emptying. So much so that the Vatican II document on liturgy speaks of her as "inseparably linked with her son's saving work" (n. 103). Mary's response to every grace bestowed on her by God was that of diminishing herself in order that God's will be fulfilled. As Andrew Gelin points out in *The Poor of Yaweh,* the Magnificat is the hymn of praise to God wherein Mary identifies herself with the *anawîm* — the poorest of the poor in the Old Testament, who had no voice, land, money or power. And in her poverty and nothingness Mary rejoices and sees that to be empty is to be beloved of God — a God whose wisdom

> puts down the mighty from their seat,
> exalts the humble:
> fills the starving with good things;
> sends the rich away empty.

Theologian Fr Chris O'Donnell points out that the Magnificat "does not stress that God has done these things in the Old Testament (as indeed he had) but that in Jesus there is a definite statement on values: wealth and power are not important in the sight of God".[6] I wonder how many of us truly believe that? I wonder how often do we convey that message to our youth? Is it any wonder that Mary means so little to us?

Mary the woman
May I conclude with what I consider to be one of the most liberating aspects of the "meditative reconstitution" regarding Mary in the Church today. That is, the rediscovery of the

womanliness of Mary. For too long I believe a lot of marian devotion and her imagistic portrayal has tended to alienate a large number of young women and indeed some men, from Mary herself. Space and time does not permit an in-depth exploration of how this came to be but a few points must be stated. Firstly I believe that a large number of popular images and epithets ascribed to Mary over the centuries particularly in our Western tradition, have tended to be really male projections of certain psychological archetypes rather than true attempts to capture the complexity and simplicity of Mary symbolically. For example, in the "courtly love" tradition of medieval times the lady — patron of the knight — was always perfect, pure, passive and *especially* unattainable. She was really a cypher, devoid of personality and placed upon a pedestal for male adoration. The psychologist Jung describes this unrealistic idealisation of the female as a compensatory process on the part of men whereby they attempt to distance, idealise and thereby cope with the unknown, i.e. woman. This idealisation model which in a sense makes a total cypher out of woman is particularly evidenced in regard to Mary when we see or hear her described as "meek", "virginal", "passive", "undefiled" — a "vessel", a "tower", a "mystical rose" while rarely do we hear or see portrayed the many beautiful womanly, *human* characteristics she possessed. (One only has to look around the various devotional statues or paintings in many churches all over Ireland to see how one sided and de-womanising our representations of Mary have been.)

One of the key points for a deeper understanding of Mary is to know her as a *woman*. She loved as only a mother can love. She suffered as a woman and a mother, and remained steadfast at the foot of the cross when many of the men (apostles) had run away. Secondly her virginity must not be distorted and understood as a negative act of abstentionist purity, which underlines the value of celibacy over and above marital union. Rather it is most clearly an *active* response to a grace from God, disposing her to be open to the fruitful loving of *all others* in the most selfless and self-emptying of ways. Thirdly Mary is not to be seen as fulfilling the stereotypical feminine role of passive receptivity. Rather her whole life, beginning with her "fiat" is a witness of *active* receptivity to the grace of God, through which, as was mentioned, she is seen as inseparably linked with her son's saving work. And this characteristic of active receptivity to the grace of God is neither an exclusively feminine or masculine preserve. Actually it is *the* single trait needed by man and woman alike if Christianity is to be lived as a meaningful reality and the Kingdom of God to begin here on earth.

A few radical feminists have attempted to assign to Mary the status of being the feminine side of God. I believe this is a very inaccurate distortion. Where Mary can be seen as "feminist" if one wants to use that word, is in her concern and identification of herself and God with the *anawîm* — those who are oppressed or dominated or treated unjustly in any way. And certainly we can see that a large part of the history of humankind can be seen as a continual process of domination and injustice perpetrated by man over woman. But in so far as this is the case men too are therefore prohibiting their own self-liberation. For men will only be fully human and truly Christian when they abandon their structures of power and domination over woman. Together we will all only be truly Christian when all types of injustice based on power and self-seeking are replaced by the true self-emptying response to the call of Christ. That call is to build a community of *equals* that sees people as *persons*, transcending accidentals such as class, colour, gender, creed, wealth and age. The Christian vision is one of resurrected humanity and there may be times in the face of such global suffering and hatred that our youth may be tempted to see it as a pipe dream. Mary once again is our symbol of hope. Mary, conceived without original sin and remaining sinless — as the New Eve — reaches back before the fall of humanity as representative of our once sinless and innocent state. In her Assumption she models for us the forward thrust of our progressive liberation to the fullness of redemption in eternal life with Christ. Mary is the true representative of a new liberated humanity for both men and women.

That liberation is the truly Christian challenge facing the young today. How to attain it? How to make the Kingdom of God on earth a reality in our day? We can look to Mary. And as we do the words of Paul VI ring clearly in our ears:

We would like to repeat that the ultimate purpose of

devotion to the Blessed Virgin is to glorify God and to lead Christians to commit themselves to a life that is in absolute conformity with his will.[7]

There can be no more profound meaning of Mary for our youth than this.

10

MARY AND THE CHURCH

† Cahal B. Daly

The Vatican Council has given us new light on what is really one of the oldest topics of Christian theology, namely the relationship between Mary and the Church. This applies primarily, of course, to the Church in the sense of the People of God, the Community of Salvation. But there is a parallelism even between Mary and the Church in the sense of a church building; and it is with this that I should like to begin.

In the liturgy of the dedication of a church, there are many scriptural readings and references which are to be found equally in the liturgy of Our Lady. The first scripture reading in the Mass of Dedication is from the twenty-first chapter of the Apocalypse. It describes:

> the holy city, and the new Jerusalem, coming down from God out of heaven, as beautiful as a bride all dressed for her husband. (*Apoc 21:2*)

It goes on:

> Then I heard a loud voice call from the throne, "You see this city? Here God lives among men. He will make his home among them; they shall be his people, and he will be their God; his name is God with them." (*Apoc 21:3*)

Now, not only can these words be used also of Mary; but, what is most important, they had first been used by the same St John, in the prologue of his Gospel, about Our Lord's Incarnation in Mary's womb. The words are very familiar to us: "The Word was made flesh, he lived amongst us". But, through translation, we miss the full force of the original meaning of the words. "Lived" is not, for St John, an ordinary banal word. It means: the Word of God "set up his tent, or his tabernacle" among his new people; as God had lived and journeyed among his pilgrim people in the Old Testament, under the sign of the golden Ark of the Covenant which was sheltered by the tent or tabernacle that accompanied the People of Israel in all their wanderings throughout their history.

It is possible that St John is in this passage consciously recalling the virginal birth of Jesus from Mary; for some scholars think that the verse before refers to the virgin birth. Our version reads:

> But to all who did accept him he gave power to become children of God, to all who believe in the name of him who was born not out of human stock or urge of the flesh or will of man but of God himself. (*Jn 1:12-13*)

But it is possible that the original and correct wording is this (which is in fact the version used by the Jerusalem Bible):

> As many as received him, he gave them power to be made the sons of God, to them that believe in *his* name who *was* born not of blood, nor of the will of man, but of God.

In other words, this would be a clear statement by St John of the virginal birth of Jesus Christ from Mary ever virgin. It was in this sense that many early Fathers of the Church understood the passage.

Ark and temple
Again, the first scripture reading in the Office of Readings for the Dedication of a Church is the description, from the Book of Chronicles, of the dedication of Solomon's temple. It tells us that, when Solomon had finished his prayer,

> fire came down from heaven and consumed the holocaust and the sacrifices; and the glory of the Lord filled the temple. The priests could not enter the house of the Lord, because the glory of the Lord filled the house of the Lord. All the sons of Israel, seeing the fire come down and the glory of Lord resting on the temple, bowed down on the pavement with their faces to the earth; they worshipped and gave praise to the Lord, for he is good, for his love is everlasting. (*2 Ch 7:1-3*)

Now these words "the glory of the Lord", have a very special meaning in the Bible. They signify the blinding cloud of mystery, at once light and darkness, darkness by excess of blinding light, which always accompanied the presence of the Almighty Eternal God. Wherever this cloud of flaming glory is, there is the one true God, the Lord of Israel. We find it above the Ark of the Covenant in the tent or tabernacle which was God's dwelling place among his people. We find it above the Holy of Holies in the temple at Jerusalem, which took the place of the tabernacle after God's people had settled in the promised land.

But what is most important for us is the presence of this same *Shekinah* or cloud of glory in the life of Our Lord. At all the important events in Our Lord's life we find the cloud, marking him as truly God, the omnipotent, invisible God of Israel, in human form. This is the New Testament's way of saying that Jesus is God. This is the New Testament truth that the Councils and creeds later express in different words, but with exactly the same content:

> God from God, light from Light, true God from true God. . . of one substance with the Father. . . .

We find this cloud of glory at our Divine Lord's Baptism, at his transfiguration, at his death on Calvary. But first we find it over Mary at the moment of the Incarnation:

> "The Holy Spirit will come upon you", the angel answered, "and the power of the Most High will cover you with its shadow. And so the child will be holy and will be called Son of God". (*Lk 1:35*)

The "overshadowing" of Mary is the appearance over her of the cloud of glory that marks the presence within her womb of God, the Lord of Israel. This is St Luke's way of telling us that at that moment God is made flesh and Mary becomes God's mother.

Mary thereby becomes the bodily Ark of the Covenant, the living temple of God, the prototype of all Christian Churches, in which again, as once in Mary's virginal body, God is present in the Mass and in the Blessed Sacrament. Actually, many of the phrases in the Litany of Loreto were first used of churches and of the Church herself. For both are, as Mary is, Tower of David, Tower of Ivory, House of Gold, Ark of the Covenant,

Gate of Heaven. We can rightly say, therefore, that the function of a church is in some sense similar to the role of Mary — to show us and give us the Blessed Fruit of Mary's womb. We can feel that the beauty of a church should be in some sense a reflection of the beauty with which Mary was adorned for Jesus, her son and her spouse. The Irish eighth-century poet, Blathmac, writes:

> How well that you bore a noble,
> summer-like being,
> Jesus, sublime, renowned; . . .
>
> You are about him, beautiful Mary,
> chosen coffer of red gold. . .

A church is, like Mary, a "chosen coffer of red gold" around the Lord who dwells within it.

It may be noted, from the examples already given, that the deeper we penetrate into the meaning and truth of Holy Scripture, the more profound and solid proofs we find for the Church's teaching about Mary. Modern scholarship, so far from weakening our faith, is instead deepening and consolidating it at every point. We shall see this even more clearly as we turn now to think of Mary in relation to the Church, the People of God.

When Pope Paul, at the close of the third session of the Second Vatican Council, proclaimed Mary as Mother of the Church, he was simply giving a new expression to a truth deeply embedded in scripture and in the oldest tradition of the Church. Almost every reference to Mary in the gospels associates her in an utterly unique manner with the salvation of the human race effected by Jesus Christ her son, and with the pouring out of saving grace from Christ upon the redeemed. The Mary of the gospels is mother and chosen associate of the Redeemer, mother and appointed mediatress of the redemption.

Annunciation and Visitation
Already at the Annunciation, every word of the angel Gabriel, when understood in its full meaning, speaks of Mary's part in mankind's salvation. For the words, as Mary herself must have related them, recall the promise of salvation renewed so often

down the centuries by the prophets. Mary knew that through her the prophecies were being fulfilled and the promised Saviour given to humanity. When the angel said: "Hail, Mary full of grace. . ." he was greeting her as representative of the new Sion, the new people of God, and announcing the coming of salvation to mankind summed up in her. For Gabriel was using words exactly parallel to those used by the prophet Sophonias to announce a coming Saviour to Sion. "Hail" is not just a form of greeting, it is a special formula for announcing salvation to Israel. Sophonias says:

> Shout for joy, daughter of Zion, Israel, shout aloud!
> Rejoice, exult with all your heart, daughter of Jerusalem.
> . . . Lord the king of Israel, is in your midst; you have no
> more evil to fear. . . . (*Soph 3:14-16*)

At the Annunciation Mary knew that Sophonias' promise of salvation was being fulfilled in her.

The scene and the words of the Visitation again point the place of Mary in the plan of salvation. They recall the Old Testament account of the bringing of the Ark of the Covenant by David from Gath to Judaea. When Elizabeth said: "Why should I be honoured with a visit from the mother of my Lord" (*Lk 1:43*) she was remembering David's words:

> However can the ark of Yahweh come to me?
> (*2 Sm 6:9*);

and she was greeting Mary as the Ark of the Lord, the New Ark of the New Covenant.

Elizabeth's greeting to Mary again recalls another scene in the Old Testament history of salvation, for it applies to Mary words first used of Judith, whom God had used to destroy the dreaded enemy of Israel, Holofernes, by cutting off his head. The King of Israel praised Judith with these words:

> May you be blessed, my daughter, by God Most High,
> beyond all women on earth; and may the Lord God be
> blessed, the Creator of heaven and earth, by whose
> guidance you cut off the head of the leader of our
> enemies. . . . The trust you have shown shall not pass from
> the memories of men, but shall ever remind them of the

135

power of God. (*Jdt 13:23-5*)

Elizabeth was recalling this scene and was greeting in Mary the new Judith, the new and true associate of the Divine Saviour of the new Israel, when she said:

> Of all women you are the most blessed, and blessed is the fruit of your womb.... Yes blessed is she who believed that the promise made her by the Lord would be fulfilled.
> (*Lk 1:42-45*)

Elizabeth's words point also, through and beyond Judith, to the first promise of salvation through a woman, which we find at the very beginning of the Bible, in the passage of Genesis which has been called the "proto-gospel":

> And the Lord said to the serpent, "Because you have done this, be accursed beyond all cattle, all wild beasts, You shall crawl on your belly and eat dust every day of your life. I will make you enemies of each other: you and the woman, your offspring and her offspring. It will crush your head and you will strike its heel". (*Gen 3:14-15*)

Calvary

The place of Mary as mother of the Church is, however, most clearly shown at the foot of the cross of Calvary. We have always known that when Christ, on the point of death, turned to Mary and said: "Woman, behold thy son"; and said to John: "Behold thy mother", Christ was really giving us all to Mary as her children and giving Mary to us as our mother. But new scripture study has given us far more solid reasons for this conviction and much deeper insight into its significance. For there is strong reason to believe that John the disciple here stands for the Church and that Mary is here being appointed by the dying Christ as mother of his Church, or, as Pope Paul was in the fullness of time to put it:

> mother of the Church, that is to say of the whole People of God, faithful of God, faithful and pastors alike.

Not long afterwards we read that Jesus bowing his head gave up his spirit (Jn 19:30). But these words too seem to have a deeper meaning, related to the preceding scene. They probably mean: "Jesus, turning his head towards his mother and the disciple, handed on the Spirit to them". In other words, the Church is now being born and the Holy Spirit is being promised to it, in the person of Mary its mother and St John. It is an Anglican theologian, Professor Eric Mascall of Oxford, who says:

> Mary and John together are the nucleus of the Christian Church and she is given to the household of the Church as its mother. To them, that is to say to the Church under the motherhood of Mary, Christ hands over the new dispensation of the Spirit.

But that is not all. The heart of the dead Christ is pierced and there pours out blood and water. St John, who saw this happen, immediately recognised that this was the giving of the promised Holy Spirit. It is from the Sacred Heart of Christ, pierced out of love for us, that flow forever upon all mankind the life-giving waters of grace, the blood of the Blessed Eucharist and the water of Baptism and the Sacraments.

The early Fathers of the Church liked to think also of the Church as being born at that moment from the side of Christ as he slept in death. For just as God formed the first mother of mankind, Eve, from the side of the first Adam, as he slept, so God forms the second and true mother of mankind, the Church, from the side of the second Adam, Christ, as he hangs dead upon the cross. But the early Church always saw Mary and the Church as interrelated and indeed in a sense theologically interchangeable. So the birth of the Church from Christ's side is also the birth of Mary as mother of the Redeemed from the pierced heart of Christ the Redeemer. Mary is the greatest gift of the Sacred Heart to the Church.

It is above all by her faith and her obedience to God's Word that Mary is the associate of the Redeemer and the mediatress of redemption. She is the mother of faith, the virgin most faithful. She lived in the darkness and struggle of faith just as we do; she is the mother of those who have not seen but have believed. Her faith has been compared to Abraham's. Just as Abraham by faith "set out without knowing where he was going" (*Heb 11:8*), so Mary set out to accept motherhood of the Man of Sorrows, set out to receive in her soul the sword of sorrow, set out to wait for her son to work out the mystery of salvation which she could not understand but believed. The whole of her spiritual life is summed up in the words:

> Behold the handmaid of the Lord. Be it done to me according to thy word.... And seeing him, (she) wondered.... And (she) understood not the word that he spoke to (her).... And his mother kept all these words in her heart.

Her faith is most like Abraham's when at the foot of the cross, she parts with her son in obedience to God's will, for the sake of us; as Abraham was ready to slay his son Isaac in obedience to God's will. Abram by his faith became Abraham, the father of multitudes, the father of believers; so Mary by her faith, becomes mother of Christian multitudes, mother of the Church, the Community of Faith. Elizabeth said to her: "Blessed is she who believed". We can go further and say: "Blessed are we because she has believed".

This too is why she becomes mother of divine grace, mother of the sacraments. Our wonderful Gaelic eighth-century marian poems by Blathmac have this verse:

> It is your son's body that comes to us
> when one goes to the sacraments;
> the pure wine has been transmuted for us
> into the blood of the son of the King.

It is again the Anglican Professor Mascall who has said:

> We can say with a new emphasis the words that, in the Genesis story, Adam said after he had tasted the food given him by the first Eve: "The woman gave me, and I did eat." For it is the very body, the human nature, which Christ took from his mother, on which we are fed in the Holy Eucharist.

The Church our mother

It is impossible to eliminate Mary from Christian theology without eliminating with her both the Incarnation and the Church. Mary's place in the Christian creed from the very beginning has been in the very same sentence in which we affirm that Jesus Christ is the Son of God. The words, "born of

138

the Virgin Mary", are essential to the affirmation that a man born at a certain time in our history and in a certain place in our world, was indeed the son whom God, in his love, sent into the world for our redemption. Without a woman, the truth of the Incarnation could not be realised and our redemption could not have been effected. The Church was led to make statements of faith about Mary, not in order to add something to her faith in Christ, but simply in order to maintain her faith in Christ.

Similarly, as the Church came to understand her own nature better, she came to see more and more resemblances between her own nature and mission and the mystery and vocation of Mary. The Church recognised herself as sharing with Mary the role of spouse of Christ, spouse of the Holy Spirit, mother of the living, mother of believers, faithful virgin. Indeed, many of the titles which came to be used of Mary in her litanies were first applied to the Church herself. The theology of the Church derived in considerable part from reflection on what is taught about Mary in the gospels; just as much of the Church's understanding of Mary derived from what is revealed in the gospels about the Church. To suppress the theology of Mary would be gravely to impair the theology of the Church.

But it is not only the theological understanding of the Church which is distorted when we neglect the role of Mary; it is also our feeling about the Church, our emotional relationship with the Church, which is damaged. Even the term, "the institutional Church", is not traditionally or natively Catholic. It is even difficult to harmonise with the instinctive Catholic language which calls the Church our mother. We do not think of our mother as "an institution". We do not have an "institution" as our mother. The late Archbishop Fulton Sheen used to say: "an abstraction does not have a mother". We cannot feel about our mother as we would about an institution. Especially, we are reluctant to engage in criticism of our mother, nor do we enjoy hearing others criticise her. We do not talk about her impersonally, as about a stranger; rather we feel part of her and feel her to be part of ourselves; we identify with her. I fear that we are in danger of coming unconsciously to adopt a wrong attitude towards the Church, because we are tending to forget that the Church is our mother; and we are coming to forget this precisely in the measure in which we are neglecting devotion to the mother of Christ and our mother, Mary. If we learned again to think, as the Church has traditionally done, about the Church and Mary together, then there could never be a note of bitterness in our feelings towards the Church or in our language about her. We could never relish criticising her or hearing her criticised; on the contrary, to hear the Church attacked would affect us in exactly the same way as it would be to listen to someone criticising our own mother.

Our relationship with the Church should be a reflection of our relationship with our own mother. Our love for the Church should correspond to our love for the Blessed Virgin Mary. Pope Paul reminds us that when devotion to Mary is safe-guarded, then "love for the Church becomes love for Mary and vice versa, since the one cannot exist without the other".

Mary and the Spirit

There is a special relationship between Mary and the Spirit; indeed between the female sex and the Spirit. It is significant that the Hebrew word for the Spirit of God, Ruah, is feminine, as is the word for the divine wisdom in Hebrew, Greek and Latin. The liturgy is not engaged in mere grammatical conceits when it uses readings from the Sapiential Books of the Bible in reference to Our Lady. The connection between Our Lady and the Holy Spirit in scripture is deep.

Mary and the Second Coming

The Holy Spirit is at work in the world, preparing the "formless void" of history for the final consummation of the new creation at the second coming of the Word, just as the Spirit "hovered over the water" at the first creation when God's word was first spoken and the first light shone. It is the same Holy Spirit who listened to the longing of Mary for the coming of the Redeemer and then "hovered over" her at the Annunciation, when the Word came in the flesh. The same Spirit listens to and utters the longing of humanity and of the whole creation for the final coming of the risen Redeemer in the glory of the consummated redemption. St Paul more than once associates the groaning of creation for its total redemption, its total liberation, with the work of the Holy Spirit.

> We groan as we wait with longing to put on our heavenly home over the other.... We groan and find it a burden being still in this tent.... This is the purpose for which God made us, and he has given us the pledge of the Spirit. (*2 Cor 5:2-5*)

> From the beginning till now the entire creation, as we know, has been groaning in the one great act of giving birth; and not only creation, but all of us who possess the first fruits of the Spirit, we too groan inwardly as we wait for our bodies to be set free. (*Rom 8:22-23*)

The groaning of creation for its final liberation in Christ has its climax in Mary, mother of the Church, who goes "through the pain of giving birth all over again until Christ is formed" in the lives of men (cf. Gal 4:19). It is pre-eminently Mary who is the bride, longing for Jesus to come again in the Spirit and with power, to renew the face of the earth.

> The Spirit and the Bride say, "Come". Let everyone who listens answer, "Come".... The one who guarantees these revelations repeats his promise: I shall indeed be with you soon. Amen, come, Lord Jesus. (*Apoc 21:17-20*)

11

THE BLESSED VIRGIN MARY IN A RENEWED LITURGY

Brian Magee, CM

The liturgical revision after Vatican II has produced a new calendar and new texts. These changes have not in any way diminished attention to Mary in the liturgy. The number of festivals in the Universal Calendar remains more or less unchanged. Some rationalisation has taken place, for example there is but one celebration now of the Sorrows of Mary instead of two. The stress in some celebrations has been re-orientated, for example the Purification of Our Lady on 2 February is now the Presentation of the Lord, and the Annunciation of the Blessed Virgin Mary is now the Annunciation of the Lord. A celebration of the Divine Maternity in October has become the Solemnity of the Motherhood of Mary replacing the Circumcision of the Lord on 1 January. This restores the oldest commemoration of Mary in the Roman Calendar. A very good commentary on these celebrations in the new calendar is to be found in Pope Paul VI's letter, *Marialis cultus.*

There are other celebrations of Mary to be found in calendars of religious communities and various regions, dioceses and shrines. These take over certain votive Masses to be found in the former Roman Missal, and allow for local popular devotion to be expressed fully. The present Missal has a collection of votive Mass formularies and recent additions include a Mass for the Holy Name of Mary, and full formulary, with Preface, for Mary, Mother of the Church. This means that there are now five proper Prefaces of Mary where before there had been just one common formulary.

The biggest addition is in the texts of the Lectionary for Mass. Here we have some thirty common readings, apart from the proper readings for specific celebrations — truly opening up the riches of the word of God in praise of Mary.

To the Missal has now been added a rich treasury of prayers, Prefaces and readings in honour of Mary when in 1987 the Sacred Congregation for Divine Worship published in Latin the *Collectio Missarum de Beata Maria Virgine* and the first twelve of these Masses were issued in English translation by ICEL. In Ireland these were published by Veritas Publications as *Collection of Masses of the Blessed Virgin Mary.*

The renewed liturgy then does give us an increase of texts and occasions for celebrating Mary. It is to be noted that the Saturday Mass of Our Lady is retained as a fixture in the pattern of the daily Mass celebrations.

But the impact of these texts is much greater because of the use of the vernacular. Today's celebrations are understood by all the faithful, no longer the preserve of the informed only.

For, in fact, devotion to Our Lady was not for the people in general a liturgical devotion, but one which took place at best concurrently with the liturgy. The festival and commemoration days were the opportunity for gatherings for popular devotions. Since the people were not actively participating, fully aware of the meaning, it was necessary to provide some help for understanding and devotion. Nowadays the liturgy should be able to do all this. If it is failing to have the same effect, or appears to fail, we have to find out why. Is it because we have not yet got to grips with a full understanding of what liturgy is about? Is it because we concentrate on a cerebral approach, a word-filled liturgy, that is slow to use the senses as popular devotion always did? What are the missing elements and how can they be integrated into liturgical celebration? More fundamentally, what really is being celebrated in a festival? And what does devotion to Mary entail? In failing to understand the real meaning of what we are about, we end up with piecemeal attempts to relate new liturgy with old devotion. We don't solve any problems by adding the Hail Mary to the Prayer of the Faithful, for example, against all the rules and tradition of the Roman Rite.

In the liturgy, Christ is really present, the work of our redemption is accomplished, the Paschal mystery is actualised. The participants in the liturgy are united with Christ's self-giving and are brought to the Father. In each celebration, we transcend time and space, and through Christ, with him and in him, we enter into the mystery we commemorate. Our celebrations of the Church's year are not nostalgic recollections of the past in Christ's earthly life, but a sacramental entering into that mystery now.

That is why the first daily festivals that Christians celebrated apart from the Sunday celebration of the Paschal mystery were the deaths of martyrs. They in a special and dramatic way entered into the mystery of the death and rising of Christ. The Church in honouring them — and later, apostles, confessors, virgins and others — is thanking the Father for the mercy shown in Christ and effective in the members of Christ's body. They have become witnesses for us, and examples of courage, perseverance and hope for us in living out our Christian lives. We do not set out to be carbon copies of them, for grace builds on nature's gifts. Because of our family communication in Christ, we can ask them to intercede for us.

The later growth in numbers and cult of the saints led to abuses of earlier understandings. There came a concentration on miracles and relics; *imitation* of them gave way to *invocation* of them in their special roles. The saints became helpers rather than intercessors. It is the apparent threat to the One Mediatorship of Christ that is attacked at the Protestant Reformation, and which makes Catholic popular devotion hold on more strongly. And while the teaching of the Church is that the saints are examples and intercessors for us, in the popular mind they are seen as specialised workers to whom we can turn when the particular need arises.

Obviously, Mary ranks high in all this development. When devotion to her began to develop after the third century the number of her feasts soon multiplied. Love and veneration of Mary received official approval. But such development had its problems. Some commentators would say that the heights of marian devotion in the mid-twentieth century did damage to the faith of young people and some thinking adults of that time.

Mary has always been seen as the example par excellence and the saint whose intercession could always be depended on. The various titles given her show her as a helper like the other saints, but in such a strong way that theological questions about her mediatorship role arose. The Vatican II constitutions on the Church and on the Liturgy, as well as *Marialis cultus*, have helped us to gain a proper perspective on the role of Mary and devotion to her. The task given us by the Council is to ensure that popular devotion harmonises with the liturgy. Our first challenge is to make liturgical festivals become in fact days of devotion. The celebration of Mass being carried out with full festivity and good, sound preaching; the Liturgy of the Hours, or alternative prayer service, being made an attractive and welcoming function. Holydays of Obligation like the Assumption and Immaculate Conception create problems especially in the cities — rushed Masses for large numbers do not conduce to devotion.

Traditional months like May and October need to be revitalised. Modern conditions of life, and other factors, make it difficult to maintain interest and freshness over protracted periods of time. Would it be better to concentrate on a week of prayer before or after the Feast of Our Lady of the Rosary in October? The sheer beauty of the May altar encourages its retention in home and church, and need not disturb the liturgical trend of Eastertide; and prayer of intercession to Mary at this time of school examinations is helpful for young people under stress. In many ways Mary's month is December as we wait and watch with her for the coming of Our Lord.

Celebrating the liturgy, keeping festival, is about recalling and deepening the meaning of an experience. We have to experience the role of Mary in the Christian dispensation, her work in the salvation of each of us, and our personal entering into that role-relationship. The liturgy is not independent of popular devotion and must itself lead to a deepening of it.

MARY IN THE IRISH TRADITION

Peter O'Dwyer, O Carm

Early texts

Writers and preachers generally consider that devotion to Mary must have found its way into Ireland in St Patrick's time since her divine maternity was defined in the Council of Ephesus in 431. Our study, however, is based on documentary evidence. The first reference to her is in a Gaelic prophecy dated c.600 in which St Brigid is called "another Mary".[1] Her divine maternity and perpetual virginity together with her close relationship with the Church are evident in Hiberno-Latin writings prior to 700.[2] The native flair is added, especially in Gaelic poetry, by Blathmac for example "Who is the fostermother who was able to nurse the suckling?" "She is the mother of the little boy who was born on Christmas night". The apocryphal influence is seen in "She read the Prophets and the Law". In the account of the Annunciation "she conceived with steadfastness and glory the well of divine wisdom". Her virginity is constantly recalled. Periodically her royal lineage is mentioned. Blathmac's poem (c.750) is his "devoted offering to Mary and her son". It seems to be a very early indication of the devotion which later solidified into the idea of the Dolours of Our Lady. Her divine maternity was accomplished by the grace of the septiform Spirit. The human and endearing touches appear periodically for example "He was more beautiful, pleasant, bigger than other boys". The word *Mairenat* (dear Mary) is a very beautiful compound. Blathmac's phrase, "Ye were sad and not sad" in Egypt shows him entering into her thoughts. The fact that Christ was crucified by his own kin, his mother's kin, was something which wounded Irish sensibilities very much. The terms of endearment like "Mary's darling" seem to occur earlier in Ireland than in Western Europe. He strikes a poignant note in the exclamation "Alas for the one who has loved the son of the king of heaven and who has seen him lying in blood". Her

mediation or intercession is clear in Blathmac's three requests
to "the little bright-necked one — the sun of women". He asks
her to get from her son a good, long life on earth and a welcome
in heaven for himself and protection from hell for all who say
the prayer as a vigil. He manifests tremendous trust in her. She
is styled "beautiful queen", "jewel" by him. He wants her to
hold converse with him — to reveal herself to him especially in
her suffering — she who is the head of pure faith. His
attestation, "You were a true virgin after the birth of Christ: he
enters pious hearts, he leaves them full and whole", is a very
deep application of the imitation of Mary and of the realisation
of the *prius mente quam ventre* of Augustine.

She is the "chosen coffer of red gold", "the shrine", "the
ark". He has the very imaginative but not over-theological
touch as he describes for her how Jesus was so welcomed into
heaven that he broke into tears. Blathmac also connects her
with the Eucharist. Her son's body is received in the Eucharist.
His body is the pledge of eternal life. The earliest instance of
this thought in the West in medieval times is found three
centuries later in Peter Damian. Another nice touch in
Blathmac's thoughtful prayer is his assurance to the mother of
Jesus that her son has risen. In his mind mother and son are
very closely unified as he concludes by telling us that final
judgement will take place before Mary's son.[3] I think that the
title *mac Maire* occurs more frequently in the early literature
than the actual name of Jesus.

Side by side with Blathmac stands Cucuimne of Iona (+747).
From the latter we learn that some monasteries sang the *Hymn
of Mary* daily. His hymn recalls that she was of the tribe of
Juda, the mother of the great Lord. She aided afflicted
humanity. Gabriel brought the Word from the Father's bosom
to Mary's womb. She is the most outstanding of virgins. This
thought will be repeated quite frequently in later writings. She
is a rock of faith. There is no other mother like her and she is
not of fully human origin. The Eve-Mary contrast appears for
the first time in Irish writing in his hymn. Through woman and
wood (i.e. the apple) the world perished — through the power
of a woman (and of the cross) it returned to salvation. Her role
with the individual Christian is seen in the statement that
"taken up by Mary we may be perfect to God". Cucuimne, like
Blathmac then makes a solemn appeal to her to save us from

147

the fire and bring us to heaven, ending his verses with the appeal to Christ to write our names with heavenly letters.[4] Cucuimne's poem is much shorter than Blathmac's. It is more succinct. Probably he was much better versed in Latin than in Irish verse. It is scriptural and theological. But it lacks the natural touch and the imagination of the Irish verse. In the prayer which follows, Mary is called "unique virgin and mother — unexampled and of singular merit whom God so preserved in mind and body", which when coupled with the words in the hymn that she was not of fully human origin, there may be an inkling of the Immaculate Conception. But we are not sure of the date of the prayer. The prayer says also that the whole world is saved by Mary. The correct relationship of Mary and Christ is evident in the poem. So Mary is obviously the secondary cause.

Her own statement that all generations would call her blest (cf. Lk 1:48) sounds a chord in Oengus, *céle Dé* (c.800). He tells us that she is praised by men and by angels. Noteworthy is the entry for 2 February, "the reception of Mary's son in the temple". The feast is one of Christ accompanied by Mary. 25 March is the Conception of Christ (the word Annunciation is not mentioned). Quite a number of feasts connected with her are commemorated i.e. the Visitation, her birthday, the Assumption, the birth of Christ from pure-white Mary. Her own conception does seem to be commemorated in the *Martyrology of Tallaght* and possibly under 3 May in the *Félire* of Oengus. From the end of the seventh or the beginning of the eighth century a feast of Mary's conception by Anne was being celebrated in the East. Its origin is linked with the apocryphal account of Mary's "active" conception by the sterile Anne. Later, attention turns to her "passive" conception due to the action of the Trinity preparing a fit habitation for the Word to become man. This feast was celebrated on 9 December and not in May, which adds further complications to the Irish entries in May.

The idea of Mary as our sister appears periodically in our early literature under various guises. The earliest reference to her in the Gaelic language is that St Brigit will be another Mary, mother of the great Lord. About 800 St Moninne is called Mary's sister. In the same work Mary is called "our sister" and this relationship is again recalled in later centuries.

The only elucidation of the idea occurs in the Notes to the *Félire* where it adds that Moninne was a virgin like Mary.[5]

Early Irish art, whether in manuscript illumination or in the figures on the stone crosses, rarely has a picture of the virgin alone or virgin with child. The *Book of Kells* has a very human representation of the mother and child but the stone crosses, if we except one in Drumcliffe, Co. Sligo, one in Iona and another in Islay, never have the virgin and child. Representations of the Crucifixion have the sponge and lancebearers but never any other attendant figures, not even the virgin or St John. On the stone crosses, Mary is found in scenes of the Nativity or of the Adoration of the Magi. The theme of the virgin or of the mother and infant does not seem to have developed until later.[6]

Ireland is the only country, to my knowledge, where a special name was gradually reserved for her i.e. (*Muire*). Personal names derive from hers e.g. (*Céle mac Maire*) before 800 and Maelmaire (tenth century), gradually increase throughout the later centuries. I have not found any church or monastery dedicated to her prior to 1100. Between that date and 1150 there are a small number but after 1150 the number increases very rapidly.[7]

Her Magnificat was frequently used and very much appreciated. Maelruain of Tallaght referred to it as the "Safe-Conduct of Mary".[8]

From 900-1100 two poems are of particular significance in the development of devotion to her. The first[9] seems to be found in only one manuscript, which suggests that it was not widely known by later generations, or that it did not appeal. The latter suggestion does not seem likely. However, it takes the form of a night-prayer of intercession in which the Queen of virgins is asked to bring the poet to heaven swiftly by her grace, to lead him by the hand. By the choice which the Trinity made of her and by the graces given to her, by her birth and by her glory he wants her to bring him to heaven. He places himself under her protection while on earth and especially at the hour of death. We have noted earlier his extraordinary plea for her protection. The devil was certainly a reality for the poet. In no other poem in this period is the plea for protection against him as strong or as frequently voiced. While the poet sees Mary as a masterpiece, he also sees her in relation to

Christi:

> Except for Christ, thou art the one most abounding in grace who has visited the world.

She has defeated the devil in battle. One wonders if this may be connected with Genesis 3:15. The imagery is very beautiful. She is the vessel in which was the manna, the shrine in which was the King of the stars, the golden cup which had the wine which gladdens and intoxicates for eternity, the paradise in which was the tree of life and her face shines like the sun. Having said all that he then returns to his original plea to save him from hell and the devil. "May it be a protection for me to praise you . . . whoever practises it rightly, may he have heaven". Blathmac had a similar request. The order of mediation is beautifully clear; "The prayer of each strong noble saint to thee; thy prayer along with each to pure Christ that I may have the gift of diligent piety always".

The second poem is one attributed to Columcille *A Maire mín, maithingen*,[10] but dating from the eleventh century. It is a plea for help and, since it is found in eight manuscripts, was very popular. Mary is called the casket of the Lord's body, the shrine of all mysteries, queen of all rulers. Once again, Mary's association with the redemption is highlighted:

> O Mary, loveliest jewel, thou hast saved our race, O truly lovely light, O garden for kings.

She is the golden coffer, the holy one from heaven, the mother of truth, victorious and strong. Christ is her father and her son. So the poet asks "Pray *with* me". Earlier Blathmac had keened *with* her. She is the choice star, the tree in bloom, a mighty torch, a sun who warms everyone, the ladder of the great fence through which the pure step into heaven, the choice door through which Christ was born. One notes the lack of prose tracts. The *Transitus* or the Assumption of Mary may have been known in Ireland in the eighth century.[11] There are Lives and tracts dating from later centuries some of which may, on further investigation, be seen to date from an earlier period. But from our knowledge of the material available at present, devotion to Mary in Ireland up to 1100 is found chiefly in poetry.

The general doctrines of the Church are clearly evident, her divine maternity, her perpetual virginity, her Assumption (though I have found no indication of bodily assumption mentioned except in the *Transitus*), her mediation or intercession which may seem a little exaggerated at times but is in correct relationship with her son. The approach to her is sometimes quite theological, at other times very deeply human. The note of protection is one of the strongest while the idea of imitation is rarely found. The figures of speech describing her are partly scriptural, partly native. Her dominant position is her protecting power which the poet implores, "I pray, while life lasts, that thou be our safeguard to the kingdom of the good Lord, and that we go with dear Jesus".[12]

Medieval times
From 1100 onwards Ireland had more contact with the Church in England and on the Continent. The reform in the first half of the twelfth century, the coming of the Cistercians c. 1142 and other Orders of monks and Canons and Canonesses, the Norman invasion and the arrival of the Mendicant Orders opened Ireland more fully to the European tradition of the spiritual life and of devotion to Our Lady.[13]

The development of the Litany is the step from the spiritual treatise to the simple prayer. *A Muire mór*[14] is a good instance of this. Donnchadh Mór Ó Dálaigh,[15] who was more probably a layman than a cleric or religious, left a deep imprint on the Irish mind and heart, e.g. "My prayer at lying-down and rising to Mary's son is that he be my path to God". Her Hours were very important to him and to many others. He describes her as the "altar of the heavenly Church".[16] Drinking from her breast causes Christ to bring him to heaven. She is his sister. To pray to her means "two-thirds of the road to heaven". She received Christ in her womb as the sun passes through glass. Donnchadh expresses in very simple words and thoughts the ideas that keep re-appearing throughout the whole period:

> Sad to my heart are the words of the woman bent over her son; God's heart softened to her weeping; her heart was dead while he was in the grave.[17]

He uses metaphors to great purpose:

> My helm on the waves is the noble lady; my mast the fair Man, as I sail from port I feel my course sure owing to them.[18]

She is the "unebbing wave" who can direct his life. He beseeches her "Be ever in my house, come into my heart, O noble Mary, and remain in it". Her influence and her power over her son stem from the fact that she is his mother, who did so much and suffered so deeply on his account. Christ's reply to her is "Anything thou wishest for thou shalt have". The fact that a bardic poem (possibly one of Donnchadh's) was on the lips of the people at the beginning of this century[19] with some additions shows the appreciation and development of confidence in her powers of intercession. So closely is she associated with the Trinity that she is at times considered almost as a member.[20] We find mention of her poverty, her nuptials and her dolours also in these poems.

Muiredhach Albanach, also a thirteenth century poet, was in touch with the apocryphal tradition as he recounts Anne's triple marriage. In his case also Mary is almost one of the Trinity.[21] Twentieth-century readers must bear in mind that this is well before the present anxieties about Mary's role entered Catholic thought (from the Reformation onwards). It may be that they looked on Mary's relation to the Trinity as the human being closest to them and co-operating with them as no other human being could. The poem, *Fuigheall beannacht brú Mhuire,* doubtfully ascribed to Giolla Brighde Mac Conmídhe, is perhaps the most outstanding thirteenth-century poem on her. It has no lengthy descriptions of her physical beauty but her spiritual role is excellently developed.[22] He may also be the author of the poem of a pilgrim to the Holy Land which says:

> I give thanks to great Mary for the flagstone which was under the virgin, the slope on which she trod is now touched by this wretched body.[23]

Another expression of a people's devotion to Mary is seen in the increasing number of churches dedicated to her from 1200 onwards. Her feasts, especially the Annunciation, the Purification, her Birthday, her Assumption and her Immaculate Conception (from the fourteenth century onwards) are celebrated. The yearly cycle, beginning on 25 March, was widely used in Ireland in the fourteenth century. Statues erected and venerated in her honour are mentioned and her Mass was regularly celebrated in cathedrals and monasteries.

The concrete expression of devotion to Mary by imitating her is voiced clearly by Gofraidh Fionn Ó Dálaigh in the middle of the fourteenth century: "Following Mary will give me knowledge of God; disobedience to her sends me astray".[24] The kinship of the poet with Mary is stressed by many of the bards but especially by Tadhg Óg Ó hUiginn (*floruit* 1450). Her three tears (of blood) are referred to more than once. She is the "tree of our wood". He strikes a very beautiful note in the thought: "To all men he is still obedient, to all women Mary is handmaid. God loves this service".[25] Mary "enticed heaven's Heir to earth". Tadhg sums up contemporary devotion to her in one of his best poems, *Tagair red Mhac a Mhuire*, when he says: "Trusting in thee 'tis scarce right for me to fear to face my fate, dread as is the judgement".[26] In the fifteenth century, appreciation of Our Lady's dolours is very evident, especially in some of the prose tracts.[27] Indications of the rosary (Mary's Psalter) also appear in this century and seem to grow much stronger in the following one.

Pilib Bocht Ó hUiginn, whose *floruit* is also mid fifteenth century, is a strong force in the development of appreciation of her and of devotion to her. This was to be expected from a "bard-friar".[28] "Lady whom God tested, chose and found good"[29] is a line of thought not often found in Continental or Gaelic literature. His approach and his confidence is deeper than that of other bards:

> Has any man, of all back to Adam, had aught to do with thee, o queen, and as a result did not cling to thee? Is there greater proof of thy sanctity?[30]

is but one example from a fine poem. The delicate touch is found in:

> Her obedience brought God's son to his mother's womb; think my friend, of the fruit it bore; 'twere good to praise Mary — lowliness reared the world's God; she was his truest nurse.[31]

He refers frequently to her humility, for example "she tested the road for us". She is the "clear short guide for souls".[32] His deep longing finds touching expression in "O blue eye, let me not — provided my passage be safe — stay here longer, as I would fain depart, my heart yearns to see you".[33] He has a keen appreciation of her virtues: "By softening the hearts of God's folk thy perfect faith saved his race from its fall till its salvation".[34] His relationship with the Trinity and with her is described as mystical espousals.[35] One great reason he has for relying on her aid is because she was so innocent and poor and had such sorrow. He has the extraordinary meaningful expression: "a draught of the well of the three streams was given her in secret". Contrast this with his very human remark: "Thy rest on Mary's soft lap saved thy race from the apple".[36] He seems to have been much influenced by the contemporary prose tracts on the Passion.

The fifteenth century saw additional churches dedicated to her. The statue of Our Lady of Trim was highly esteemed and visited by many pilgrims.[37] Wax lights burned perpetually before her statues. Reports of miracles were noted. Girdles and croziers, mitres and seals bearing representations of her are an indication of the devotion of bishops and communities to her. Guilds in her honour existed in the fifteenth century, possibly earlier. The use of her name especially in ejaculatory prayer must have been very widespread if one may judge from the marginalia on manuscripts.

It was only natural that the Irish mind, like most others, was attracted by the apocrypha. Martin MacNamara, MSC, says that "what they have to offer is a wealth of material which helps to supplement the very meagre information provided by the New Testament"[38] on certain aspects of the people mentioned in its pages. On the whole, they were used judiciously and to good purpose as the Passion-play at Oberammergau still does today. Lives of Our Lady were popular to judge from the number of copies made of them. Further studies in this field will show how much these Lives influenced the bards and will also indicate how widely they were known to the ordinary people. The fourteenth and fifteenth centuries saw great interest in all aspects of Our Lady's life, not least in her situation during the Passion of her son and after his Ascension. The influence of a work such as *Smaointe Beatha Chríost*[39] must have been enormous. To my knowledge it is the most popular text in this whole period and is also one of the better balanced, making judicious use of apocryphal and medieval literature. The influence of the *exempla* gathered under the heading of *Miracles of Our Lady* was probably fairly deep round the beginning of the sixteenth century.[40] Aongus Fionn Ó Dálaigh says: "More numerous than the leaves or blades of grass on a lawn are the tales about Mary".[41] In these, in particular, we find indications of a certain imbalance, at times, in devotion to Mary.

Sixteenth-century bardic devotion to her is beautifully exemplified in Muirchertach Ó Cionga:

> Borne on a wind of love and having the eagerness of desire in his strong wings, the Lord with one swoop entered as a sunbeam into the virgin's womb; 'twas a meeting of love and princely converse. In her kin-love she freed us from the bond of the first sin; sinless ever, ever a maid, she won her heart's darling to be her spouse. Her breast with its unquenchable flame (of love) satisfies the wrath of her son; soon shall come the hour of that satisfying, and she shall gather the six Hosts to him. Mary's wide-extending love is as the growth of a fresh-broken field, to bring all her race into one home is the marvellous achievement of her breast.[42]

Fearflatha Ó Gnímh's poem *mo-ghéanar cheanglas cumann bainríoghna*, (c. 1550-1600), though short, is a fine combination of her spiritual and natural attractions.[43] It belongs to the period where we get the short, succint bardic poems to her. An unknown bard (probably sixteenth century), in giving expression to his deep trust in Mary, ends on this note:

> She has made straight the way to heaven for me; every woman rejoices to have her kinsfolk near her; she has prepared the road for all to follow her; a stranger needs guidance.[44]

The anthology of Aongus Fionn Ó Dálaigh has seventeen poems dedicated to her. One of them has this lovely opening: "Mary, take this hand in yours". Bergin's remark that "in his religious verse he (the bard) expressed his contrition, his gratitude to his heavenly benefactors and his longing for spiritual blessings, with the same loving care and perfection of style as he did for his earthly patron" is very much to the point.[45] Mary brings his ship to shore "against an angry tide". One of his most popular poems is the one which begins *Soightheach balsaim brú Muire* (Mary's womb is a vessel of balsam).[46] The modern psychiatrist should find this interesting. In a later poem he says: "All thy members are but the cover of a

heart that has no fleshly sin".[47] The phrase describing her as
"our guiding wand" is very dear to Aongus.[48] He also remarks
that so much has been said of Mary that it is hard to find new
ideas about her but we should note that he felt the need to keep
expressing the old ideas in different ways as an outlet for his
devotion. Her "gentle ways can save him". His poems are a
séad suirghe ("gem of love") for her. Her role is well expressed
in the words: "Mother of steadfast faith, she bore her son
owing to her graces. She won possession of us by her
Annunciation. In her holy wisdom she conceived God's plan".
The natural phrase comes to him with great facility: "Thou
whose knee nursed the faith".[49] For him

> Mary is the mother of the King; the guide of his soul, the
> boat that leads to everlasting life; the greatest of all
> women.[50]

He has some unusual titles for her. She is the "lady-physician
without equal" and "the wife of the King of the Passion".

Poets like these were men who had a deep spiritual life into
which their devotion to Mary fitted quite naturally. While
Continental exaggerations found their way into some of the
compositions the indications are that there was a very deep
living devotion manifest not only in literature and in churches,
guilds and shrines but in the lives of men like Aodh Rua Ó
Domhnaill, the Mac Suibhnes of Fánaid and Bishop MacBrien
of Emly, to name but three who exercised considerable
influence in the closing years of the sixteenth century.[51]

Counter-Reformation period
It was to be expected that the efforts of the reformers to
proscribe the Mass, devotion to Our Lady and the saints
especially in the seventeenth and eighteenth centuries were
bound to affect the spiritual life of the Irish people. Ignorance
of the truths of religion resulted inevitably from lack of
preaching. Attendance at Mass could be at best but spasmodic,
prayer however was always possible and at this time the people
seem to have taken the rosary very much to heart. When
Fearghal Óg mac an Bháird went to Scotland around the year
1600 in search of wealth he found neither Mass nor clergy
there. He prayed to Christ and noble Mary, "Éire's fond
hope", that he would be able to return to Ireland. Flann mac

Conmídhe, probably a contemporary of Fearghal Óg's, has an excellent description of her relationship with us.

The life-work of those blue eyes in her rosy face is to watch over us; for love of us she bore her son, this lady ever-virgin, this shaft piercing all hearts with her charms.[52]

When Tuileagna mac Torna Ó Maolchonaire abjured his submission to the new religion around 1600 and came to Lough Derg to do penance he besought Mary to watch over his vigil.[53] The imbalance regarding Mary's power over her son is still found periodically. "If you are thinking of retribution from your people, you will not get half of it. Remember you are Mary's son, your blood is not wholly your own".[54]

Though the reign of Queen Mary (1553-8) allowed outward manifestation of devotion to Our Lady, and the Sodality of the Blessed Virgin was founded by the Jesuits in 1565, Archbishop Dermot O'Hurley was put to death in 1584 and Sir John Burke of Brittas was imprisoned in Dublin Castle in 1603. It is interesting to note that he recited the Little Office of Our Lady and the rosary constantly as he prepared for his death. The years 1560-1600 seem to be the decades when the rosary became widely practised in Ireland. Statues of Our Lady, such as Our Lady of Holy Cross, Our Lady of Limerick and Our Lady of Waterford, were held in high esteem and in 1650 she was proclaimed patronness of Ireland under the title of her Immaculate Conception. This was also the century that witnessed the introduction of the Catholic catechism, printed in Gaelic. Through it the doctrinal and devotional aspects of the cult of Mary were set out clearly. It is very likely that these catechisms were the backbone of preachers' sermons at least in the Gaelic parts of the country. Her seven joys and seven sorrows were well-known to the people. The pilgrimage to Our Lady's Island in Wexford was in vogue in the seventeenth century.[55]

The Act of 1697, which banished the bishops and regular clergy and many of the secular priests, imposed severe restrictions on the parochial clergy who were allowed to remain. But devotion to Our Lady always continued. A text such as *Parliament na mBan* written in 1697 (MS 1373 TCD), compiled between 1703-10, shows a great interest in devotion to Our Lady. Well-known poets such as Séamus Dall

157

macCuarta (d. 1733) and Séan Ó Neachtain (d. 1728) are good instances of the literary man's approach to her, their appreciation of her feasts and hymns. She is, for them, the ground of hope for better times for the country. She is described as the spouse of priests, "the guide of all generations" who is capable of vanquishing the Saxon. As *Trom do chodla a Mhuire mhór* complains:

> Heavy is your sleeping, great Mary. Do you not hear young and old and the clergy crying and appealing to you ceaselessly and yet no action or account is being made of their suffering.[56]

Seán Ó Neachtain's son, Tadhg, has a translation of the *Ave maris stella (Réalt na mara fáilte)* in his manuscript, Egerton 198, which is dated as 1717. Tadhg also shows his ability to translate Irish poems into Latin poesy (TCD MS 1361, 225-7). Printed sermons and poems from the first half of the eighteenth century often refer to Mary's part in her son's passion. They frequently use ideas found in *Smaointe Beatha Chríost*.

The belief in and devotion to her Immaculate Conception was widespread in Ireland in the century preceding its definition in 1854. Her roles as mediatrix and protectress became more pronounced. The prayer *Sgíathlúireach na Maighdine Muire* (i.e. her protective armour) was well-known and used as a plea for protection. Prayers and offices to her are very common in the eighteenth century and imitation of her virtues is highly recommended. Any priest who changed his religion betrayed Mary, his spouse. By contrast a poet such as Cathal Buí mac Giolla Gunna (+c. 1756), who had his periods of waywardness, could plumb the depths of sorrow and repentance and make his final appeal to her:

> My race is run — my time is short. My lot is sad with my sins noted against me. But I beseech you, Mary, nurse and mother of the son of God, that my body may requite all the evil which I have done.[57]

Piaras mac Gearailt, who changed his religion to save his family from starvation, gave expression to his belief in Our Lady's goodness in the poem *Tréithe na Maighdine* (1762). To Tadhg Gaelach must go the accolade for popular religious song in the second half of the eighteenth century. Two of his most frequently quoted lines are:

Soillse na Maighdine agus grása an Uain
go bhfaghamna mar oidhreacht 'na árus buan
(May the light of the virgin and the grace of the Lamb
be our inheritance in his eternal home).

The people of the Pale (an area around Dublin under British control) were very conversant with English in the eighteenth century so it is not surprising to find spiritual books, written in England, making their way across the channel. In time Irish writers such as Bishop Anthony Coyle published the *Pious Miscellany* (1787-8). The publications have sections which treat of Our Lady. The Brown Scapular devotion spread more widely in the eighteenth and nineteenth centuries. Indications that it had great vogue and that it was valued for its protective power may be seen in the fact that the Irish and the French soldiers used it as a sign of recognition in the 1798 rising and in the many applications by the clergy for faculties to enrol people in it.[58] A few sermons (one on her Annunciation, and one on her Assumption) probably date from this period also.[59]

Pádraig Denn, the sacristan-poet and successor to Tadhg Gaelach, turns to Mary and asks her to intercede for him, a sinner, and to fill his heart with love for her son. His contemporary, Mícheál Ó Longáin, gives an excellent description of her relationship with the Trinity:

Most outstanding of the women of the world, the Father chose her as his ward (child?) before all others; the Son chose her as his mother out of love; and the Holy Spirit chose her as his loving spouse.[60]

Devotion to Mary travelled with the Irish convicts and emigrants to Australia in the beginning of the nineteenth century. In Ireland it found wider expression in May devotions and processions, in the fact that the new native Orders, e.g. the Presentation Sisters, the Little Company of Mary, had a special dedication to her, in the spread of devotion to the Sacred Heart of Mary, and in novenas for her feasts and confraternities established to honour her. Daniel O'Connell had a deep devotion to her which he showed in reciting his rosary quietly in the precincts of the Westminster Parliament, in his predilection for the *Stabat Mater* and the *Memorare* and

159

in his gratitude to the Irish people for the Novena to Our Lady for her birthday, 8 September 1844, which was offered throughout the country for his release from prison.[61]

Her feastdays, if they were not holidays of obligation, were days of special devotion. Churches were more frequently named in her honour. The proclamation of the dogma of her Immaculate Conception in 1854 led to festive celebrations throughout the country and to a number of pastoral letters on the subject from Cardinal Cullen of Dublin. Numerous churches, convents, schools, which were built at this time, used this special title as their dedicatory name.[62] Various appearances of Our Lady, especially the manifestation at Lourdes in 1858, served to increase the interest of the ordinary people in the dogma and in the rosary. From the middle of the century excellent prayerbooks of considerable length included novenas and hymns and other devotions to her. The English language was better known in the country by this time, and religious houses especially convents and parochial missions, did much to make devotion to Mary a part of every home.

It is very difficult to gauge what effect the apparitions at Knock, Co. Mayo, in 1879 had on the country as a whole until quite recent times. Gaelic poetry still continued its old tradition in her regard. An unknown poet maintains that medieval approach:

> An unlearned poet finds it hard to praise you, room of heaven, mirror of glory, unbroken, glass, coffer of solace, pearl, created by the King of heaven with great respect.[63]

The simplicity and effort at total commitment expressed by the poets tend to be passed over too lightly:

> I give my soul to you, King of the Sunday and I shall never, never ask it back. You are my witness, queen of mercy, that I have left my soul with your son.

More touching because of the stark reality of experience is the prayer of the wives of fishermen:

> They are leaving us, o star of the sea, guard them all from the danger of the boats. Be with them until they return across the bar (sea) — and, O virgin, you have our eternal gratitude.[64]

We have evidence that the rich tradition of devotion to Mary was filtered through to the ordinary Irish people in the large number of prayer-poems published in *Ár bPaidreacha Dúchais*[65] and in the tales, practices and prayers which speak of her in our folk traditions published in *Béaloideas*.

Archbishop Cunnane's insight into the relation of faith and devotion serves as an opportune and valuable conclusion.

> Devotion needs the continual check of faith if it is not to degenerate into superstition or sentimentality. And theology — particularly the theology of Mary — must keep its eyes always on devotion, not only to approve or condemn, but sometimes too to learn from the subtler reasoning of the living Church what its own syllogisms could never teach it.[66]

13

MARIST MARIAN HERITAGE

Romuald Gibson, FMS

Let me begin my presentation of the Marist marian heritage by telling you a story. . . a tale so old and so often told in many forms that the names of the people involved have been forgotten.

The story tells of a holy man coming out from his mountains of contemplation, down towards a village in the valley. As he approached the village, a peasant came running to meet him.

"Are you come out of the hills?" he asked the holy man breathlessly; "Oh, if you are, then give me the stone, please give me the stone."

"Stone?" said the traveller. "What stone?"

"The stone of my dream", said the peasant. "Oh, please give it to me!" He drew breath a little and then went on: "Last night, an angel of the Lord spoke to me in a dream, telling me that today a holy man would come out of the hills and that he would give me a stone that would make me rich beyond my wildest hopes. All morning I have waited and watched. . . and now, you have come. You must give me the stone. . . it is mine. . . I have been given it by the Lord".

"Ah", said the holy man, "you must be talking of the stone that I picked up back in the mountains", and he rummaged among his few possessions. "Yes, here it is. Take it, my friend, and be glad", and he handed over a stone as big as a man's fist.

The peasant took it in trembling hands, and his eyes grew wide with wonder: "But. . . but. . . this is a diamond! Surely the largest diamond in the world!" he gasped.

"Yes, it is a diamond" said the holy man, "and now it is yours; may it bring you gladness, since the Lord has meant it for you".

The peasant, clutching his treasure in both hands turned and sped back to the village, his feet scarcely touching the ground. And the holy man settled down in the shelter of a tree, and drank in the beauty of the ordered valley, after the weeks he had spent among the mountain harshness.

As evening drew on, a figure emerged from the village, and with slow steps climbed up towards the tree; it was the peasant to whom the holy man had given the diamond. He came and sat down beside the holy man, and for a long time neither of them spoke. Finally the peasant reached into his pouch, took out, unwrapped and put the diamond on the ground between them.

"Here is the stone", he said; "now I want something more from you. . . something greater. . . give me what you have. Give me the power to give away such treasure, freely, gladly, without regret. Give me that freedom, that spirit which you have".[1]

This story has its point when we come to consider our Marist marian heritage because, being asked to speak of this, we are asked to go beyond the work we do in the Church. . . the work of schools, hospitals, parish work, missions. . . all the multiple ministries that Marists are engaged in. . . to the spirit that underlies and gives life to them all. The work we engage in is, in a sense, the stone we give, that others might be enriched; but what enables us, indeed impels us to give this stone, this ministry to the needs of the Church? This question brings us into touch with the Marist spirit, the animating presence of Mary, the inner heart of the Marist congregations. It is my privilege and my pleasure to share with you this element of the Marist charism that is so dear to us.

For those unfamiliar with Marist history, let me say that the Society of Mary arose out of the enthusiasm of a group of young French seminarians who came to believe that it was the Blessed Virgin's wish to found a society which would bear her name; she herself would be its foundress, and she would share her own spirit with its members.

This conviction arose out of a remarkable event at the marian shrine of Le Puy, in central France. Here, on 15 August 1812, a young Frenchman, Jean-Claude Courveille, while praying before the statue of Mary and the Child, heard these words spoken within his heart:

> What I want is this: since in everything, I have imitated my divine son, and followed him even to Calvary, standing at the foot of the cross while he gave his life for the human race, now that I am in glory with him, I imitate

him still in whatever he does for his Church on earth, this Church whose protectress I am, like a powerful army ranged to defend it and to save souls:

since, in the times when a terrible heresy was overwhelming Europe, Jesus inspired his servant Ignatius to found a society which would bear the name of Jesus, would be called the Society of Jesus whose members would be known as Jesuits pledged to fight against the evil unleashed against the Church of my divine son —

therefore, I want (and this is the wish of my adorable son) that, in these last days of unbelief and impiety, there be also a society consecrated to me, which will bear my name and be called the Society of Mary, whose members shall be called Marists, to fight the battle against evil. . .[2]

As a student at the seminary of Lyons, Courveille, four years later, shared this revelation made to him with other seminarians, who, in their turn, became fired with the desire to establish this Society of Mary. They saw the Society as having three branches — Marist Fathers, Marist Sisters, and a "Third Order" of lay-people. In actual fact, this plan of a "tree with three branches" failed to encompass the vitality and diversity of the Marist life that developed. In addition to the three branches originally planned, three other initiatives sprang forth:

— the Marist Teaching Brothers, or "Little Brothers of Mary";
— the Marist Co-adjutor Brothers;
— the Missionary Sisters of the Society of Mary.

Although it was Jean-Claude Courveille who carried the message at first, it fell to others to establish the first Marist groups:

— in 1817, Marcellin Champagnat founded the Marist Teaching Brothers;
— 1817 too, saw the first steps being taken towards the founding of the Marist Sisters by Jeanne-Marie Chavoin;
— from 1817 Father Jean-Claude Colin worked to set up the Marist Fathers, who received papal approbation in 1836;
— Françoise Perreton and the women who followed her,

in 1845, launched the beginnings of an extraordinary group of missionary women who, in 1931, became approved as the Missionary Sisters of the Society of Mary.

Each of these Marist branches operates now as a separate congregation having its own autonomy and identity; nevertheless, the fact that the various groups arose out of a common inspiration, that they have shared a linked history, and that they possess a common spirit, is a bond of union and a basis for collaboration that is becoming increasingly common in our own day. In 1983, at Fribourg in Switzerland, we had the experience of a four-months course in which Marist Fathers, Marist Sisters, Marist Missionary Sisters and Marist Brothers lived and shared together the work of renewal in the religious life; it was fascinating and enriching to share the insights into the fundamental Marist charism which each of the Marist groups had developed, to share what we held in common and what particular elements of the common charism each of the congregations had stressed and especially developed.

It is from this common inspiration that I wish to draw when speaking of the Marist marian heritage. Rather than confine myself to the history of any one of the Marist groups, I would like to attempt to share with you, the charism common to us all — and so I shall be referring mainly to the men and women who drew together the first Marists, the priests who founded the Marist Fathers and the Marist Teaching Brothers, and the woman who established the Marist Sisters, referring to all three rather than to any one of them, for it was these three —

Blessed Marcellin Champagnat,
Fr Jean-Claude Colin,
Sr Jeanne-Marie Chavoin,

the founding people, who, in their interpretation of the Blessed Virgin's call, laid down for us the essential elements of the Marist marian heritage.

When we focus in on this marian heritage given to the Marists, what emerges from the past is perhaps not what we might reasonably expect of a society that bears the title of the "Society of Mary". The Marists have made no great contribution to theological or mystical studies concerning Mary, the mother of God. They have published little about her. They promulgate no special form of devotion to her that is in any way akin to the rosary cherished by the Dominicans, or the scapular of the Carmelites, or the Perpetual Succour devotion of the Redemptorists.

What then is the Marist marian heritage? Perhaps it can be summed up in these two points:

(a) a deep sense of Mary present and active in the Church today — the Mary of Nazareth and the Mary of Pentecost;

(b) the understanding that the Marist is to co-operate with Mary in such a way that, in the Marist, Mary's presence, her work and her spirit are to be brought home to Christian awareness today.

Let us look at these summary points in some detail.

Mary active in the Church

From their own lived experience, Marists have a sense of Mary as a woman who is actively present[3] in their own lives, who is present to and active in the life of each Christian.

It took me a long time to appreciate the full import of this seemingly simple statement. From my mother's knee, I was taught that Mary is a gracious woman, who, out of her concern for me, would intercede with God for me; and that she is a woman to be revered and imitated. She was the Lady on the pedestal, the Queen enthroned, kindly and gentle, but for all that, Lady and Queen removed from me, awaiting my approach to her. But the Marist founders discovered that, far from being distant and exalted, she is a woman who walks with us and works among us, a woman who quits her pedestal and her throne to be our companion. Rather than awaiting our approach to her, she takes the initiative, reaching out with untiring intent to bring to reality among us, the reign of her son, Jesus Christ. Only slowly did I come to understand how strongly and immediately did the Marist founders experience this "active Mary" in their own lives.

To them, the very idea of the Marist society was hers;[4] it was Mary who took the initiative and established such a society. It was *her* work. . . she was the foundress. . . she chose the men and women who would be Marists,[5] and, to mark her initiative, she gave this group her own name. She was and always is the superioress of all Marists... their leader, inspiring, animating, guiding, urging, encouraging, comforting.[6]

To have such an understanding of Mary is to bring her alive in the Church in quite a new way. Long-standing tradition has pictured her as:

— a solace in time of need, the gentle and understanding woman who is ready to intercede for sinners with her son and Lord;

— and as the perfect woman, the perfect Christian, the model of all Christian virtues.

These are valuable and precious insights, and the tradition that enshrines them is alive and vibrant in the Church today,[7] immensely benefiting the lives of Christians.

Yet, to remain here and not to go further, is perhaps to limit and confine Mary. . .to stereotype her. . .and through her, to stereotype unwittingly the role of Christian women. Mary — and the Christian woman — can be restricted to the role of comforter, intercessor, a woman warm and concerned but docile and submissive, quiet, unobtrusive; this, I feel, is to do less than justice to the role that the Lord has assigned to Mary and to the Christian woman.

What the Marist founders grasped. . .and what ultimately penetrated through to me. . .is that this woman, Mary, is an active and dynamic lady; she is not only the queen, in glory clad, in the palace up yonder, but she is also here beside us in the marketplace, sleeves pinned back, energy in every line of her, cheerfully prepared that her skirts be bedraggled in the comings and goings of work. To the founding Marists, it was not so much they who sought her help, as she asking help of them, calling for their time and talents and dedication to aid her in spreading Christ's kingdom. She was the fire, they the branches, that Christ might stand illuminated before all people. Or, to use an image of one of your own poets, where he writes:

> O glorious virgin. . . .
> There is no music so gentle,
> Or praise so pleasant,
> Nor in the hearing of ears
> Is there a voice so fair
> As the gentle sound of you,
> My mountain stream,

And you coming from high above
As a full spring of life.[8]

"Mountain stream". . .alive, vital, purposeful, drawing into its impetuous flow the other wandering rivulets, adding their force to its own. . .yes, this is how the Marist sees Mary, and, caught up in the current of her action within the Church, we are called to work alongside her, blending our energies with hers.

In our marian heritage, two scriptural presentations of Jesus' mother embody our concept of what is her work within the Church. Our founding Marists are forever directing us to

(i) Mary at Nazareth;
(ii) Mary at Pentecost,

and I wish to treat briefly of the understanding they had of each of these images.

1. Mary at Nazareth

Dwell with me for a few moments on the thought of Nazareth. . . the village sheltered by the Galilean hills. . .the daily round of village life. . .Mary, the village girl and Joseph, the young carpenter. . .Jesus, the child, the boy, the young man, there "growing" as Luke tells us, "in body and mind, growing in the love of God and in the love of those who knew him".[9]

What was the life of Mary at Nazareth. . .what was her action there? Beyond the routine of the housewife's tasks, the responsibilities of being wife and mother, what was she trying to do?

It was at Nazareth that Mary's involvement in the life of Jesus began. There, in the mystery of the Annunciation, she becomes the God-bringer, the woman pregnant with the Word of God. Through her, he comes among us, the God-Man, the Messiah. From the Nazareth moment of her welcome:

Oh, yes! Let it be done to me as you have said![10]

her whole life revolves around Jesus, around bringing Jesus to the world. So Fr Colin could say:

Look at the Blessed Virgin. See how she hastened the coming of God by her burning desire. When she learnt that she had been chosen to be his mother, what efforts she made to co-operate! When Jesus Christ was born, he was the object of all her thoughts and affections. After his

death, her sole thought was the extension and develop-
ment of the incarnation. That is the sign precisely, by
which you can recognise a Marist.[11]

This was Mary's mission at Nazareth; this *is* Mary's mission
today in the Church — to bring Jesus to the world, to bring the
world to Jesus. She is the *Christ-bringer* now, as she was when
she brought him to Elizabeth and Zachary, to the shepherds at
Bethlehem, to the temple of his Father, to Egypt, to Cana's
wedding guests. Joseph Campbell, poet of the North and of
Wicklow appreciated this; in one poem he salutes Mary as:

> Glorious child-bearer,
> secret womb. . .
> the white love of the Gael;[12]

and in another, *The Lost Child*, he has her whispering:

> Sionan, my sorrow,
> The mother is here,
> Come unto Christ
> Who'll make you a star
> To dream in the dusk
> When summer is fair.[13]

The child-bearer, the Christ-bringer, she who urges "Come
unto Christ", the "circle of whose arms has changed the world
to a cradle for God"[14] — this mission of Mary at Nazareth is
what she would share with her Marists. To be with her in this,
to be Christ-bringers to the world, is the primary task of the
Marist. Champagnat sums up the mission of the Marist
Brother as:

> To love Jesus Christ, to work to make him known and
> loved, is the whole aim of our vocation and the purpose of
> this institute.[15]

And Colin expresses the same thought when he says:

> What a marvellous vocation, what a moving mission you
> have received. . .to form Jesus Christ in hearts and minds.
> . . to sow within people the seeds of eternal destiny.[16]

It is not as though Mary, in gathering her Marists together,
wishes to keep them to herself. To quote again from Cham-
pagnat:

> Mary keeps nothing for herself; when we consecrate ourselves to her, she accepts us only that she might give us to Jesus and fill us with Jesus.[17]

Christ-bringer to us, Mary enlists us in her work of being Christ-bringer to all.

> "It is Mary", says Fr Colin, "who gives each one his task. . . just as her divine son entrusted a mission to his apostles, calling them his friends and telling them to go and to teach all nations . . . just so this kind mother says to us: 'Go and proclaim my divine son to the world. I am with you. Go, we shall still be together'."[18]

To be a Christ-bringer to the world is, of course, the task of every Christian — each of us, you and I, have this mission from our baptism into Jesus. This task of every Christian, in the case of the Marist, is seen to be done *with Mary*, as a co-worker with her, sharing in her deepest yearnings, drawing enthusiasm from her — hence a sense of not being alone in bringing the Lord to people; Mary is at hand, she guides and supports the work.

From Mary and Nazareth stems another and vital aspect of the Marist marian heritage, an aspect that is expressed consistently and continuously in our tradition as "being hidden and unknown". Jeanne-Marie Chavoin, speaking to her Sisters says — and her words are typical of the Marist founders —

> Let us love to be hidden and unknown in this world, as Mary was, since we wish to be her daughters.[19]

This sense of Jesus, Mary and Joseph living the quiet village life in despised Nazareth, unknown, unregarded by the important people in high places, hidden from public attention, yet profoundly benefiting the world by their loving obedience to the Father's will, and by the humility, simplicity and modesty of their lives. This sense of the "Nazareth approach" deeply colours the Marist apostolate. To the early Marists, it emerges as a key element in Mary's way of bringing Jesus to people:

— she never claimed the limelight of attention;
— she never sought public approval or praise;
— she was never one for display or show or fanfare.

Good must be done; Jesus must be brought to people — but in ways that leave the focus of attention on him, and not on those who bring him. The Christ-bringer, like Mary, is to be hidden and unknown, content that Jesus be known, acclaimed, loved and served.

This marian characteristic of doing good quietly, without fuss or parade, was eminently adapted to the times in which the founding Marists lived. All three of them had lived through the tumult and danger of the French Revolution where the mighty and the prominent people were struck down, where notable works of the Church attracted hostility and vehement opposition. Direct and public confrontation of the evils that beset France in the post-revolutionary times — the immorality, the violence, the espousal of a liberty that rejected any form of direction, the materialism, the incessant and ruthless struggle for power, the strident anti-clericalism — direct confrontation of these, the Marist saw, would only inflame the hostility that smouldered there. There was no good to be gained in trying to fight fire with fire. No, the way to win souls in such a tense situation was Mary's way, with gentleness, understanding, mercy, with the simplicity and humility that she showed when she brought Jesus to people. What was needed was a quiet, unassuming yet dynamic apostolate in a de-Christianised society, an apostolate "hidden and unknown", yet like Mary's, completely committed.[20]

A recent poem by Eamon Mac Craoidhe captures something of this Nazareth element in Mary:

> Gentle woman who walked very humbly
> On the road through the glen
> Of confused noise,
> Taking no pride in your polished shoe
> But keeping your eye
> On where you placed your foot;
> Who never stumbled
> Over the rocky stone of straying,
> Nor minded the cutting wind
> Blowing from the North
> Upon your face;
> Who felt the showers of want and blame,

> But didn't step in the pools of shame;
> Hear my prayer, and
> May it not be swept away with the wind.[21]

The poem is a praise of Mary's hidden and unknown way, of her gentleness, her humility, of her "taking no pride", of her accepting blame and want and seeking no praise, yet moving forward, sure footed, valiant of heart.

Yet one more element of the life at Nazareth emerged as contributing to the Marist spirit. It is this — from the life of the Holy Family there, the founding Marists came to realise the importance of the contemplative dimension for their men and women, who, engaged in an active ministry, could easily become engrossed in the work, and neglect the continuing personal search for God that is so essential to the work, if it is to be in truth a bringing of Christ to people.

Fr Colin sums this up well when he says:

> In all things let us look to Mary, let us imitate her life at Nazareth. . .we must have the spirit of Mary, humble and hidden. . .let us therefore unite silence and prayer with action. The Society of Mary desires that we, Mary's children, should be missionaries of action and missionaries of prayer.[22]

Thus the image of Mary of Nazareth brings to our heritage the presence of the Christ-bearer, Mary hidden and unknown yet dynamic, a woman blending harmoniously together contemplation and action. Hopkins could write:

> Christ our Saviour still
> . . .makes, O marvellous!
> New Nazareths in us,
> Where she shall yet conceive
> Him, morning, noon and eve;[23]

Such poetry might be beyond our founders, but they would welcome his expression of something that was deep and vital to them.

2. Mary at Pentecost and in the early Church

The second image that the early Marists drew on was that of Mary at Pentecost and in the early Church. The Pentecost scene, described by Luke in the opening chapter of the Acts of the Apostles, is familiar to us all. After the ascension of the Lord,

> they went back to Jerusalem, to the upper room where they were staying... and all joined in continuous prayer, together with several women, including Mary, the mother of Jesus, and with his brothers.[24]

The scene is a vivid one — the infant Church grouped in prayer, with Mary in the midst, awaiting the coming of the Spirit who would set their hearts on fire and send them forth to proclaim the "good news" of Jesus.

The role of Mary in these beginnings of the Church spoke strongly to the Marist founders. Colin frequently falls back on the original revelation made to Courveille at Le Puy, where he understood Mary to have said:

> I was the support of the new-born Church;
> I shall be its support at the end of time.[25]

He describes Mary as the light, the counsel, the consolation of these first disciples of Jesus, as the guide of the apostles, their inspiration and comforter.[26]

In our own day — and this points to the relevancy of our marian heritage — Pope Paul VI stresses the same presence of Mary in the infant Church, speaking of her as —

> a woman whose action helped strengthen the apostolic community's faith in Christ.[27]

As in Nazareth, Mary's presence in the first Christian community is discreet, selfless, unassuming, still "hidden", still little known, yet strong and effective. It is in this situation that Mary's action takes on a new dimension; now, she begins a new ministry to the Church — it is this — *she shares with Christ's followers her way of responding to the Lord.* Whereas her role as Christ-bringer has her presenting us with Jesus, the Saviour, now her task as "support to the new-born Church" has her showing the Christian how he must respond to the Lord. In Bethlehem and Nazareth she brings forth Jesus and taught him to be human; now she mothers forth the Christian, teaching him to heed the divine. Again, Pope Paul VI comments on this: he writes,

> Mary is the teacher of the spiritual life for individual Christians.[28]

The early Marists had a dream — an impossible dream, you might say, or even an egoistic one: they dreamt of a whole world become Marist.

> "Our aim", said Colin, "is nothing less than to make the whole world Marist."[29]

Talking to Cardinal Castracane, Colin found himself challenged on this point:

> "Make the whole world *Marist*?" queried the Cardinal.
> "Oh yes, Eminence," Colin assured him; "You yourself could be a Marist, and the Pope himself — he would be our head".[30]

There is no record of the Cardinal eagerly following up the invitation, and well might he express surprise. What did the little French priest mean in speaking of a whole world made Marist? Was this a design to usher into oblivion the whole glorious array of Franciscans, Ursulines, Dominicans, Jesuits, Carmelites, etc. to make way for a uniform and all-pervading Maristness? The truth was much less dramatic or sinister. To "make the whole world Marist" was the Marist way of expressing their conviction that if the Church is to become what in reality is — the virgin bride of Christ and the mother of believers — then the Church must become more and more like Mary.

Their thinking ran thus:

— Mary, from being Jesus' mother, becomes his first and perfect disciple, i.e. she makes the perfect human response to him and to the Spirit he sends;

— therefore, every other follower of Jesus needs to look to her for guidance in becoming a true disciple of the Lord, needs to learn from her what true discipleship means and how it is to be lived;

— i.e. each Christian, if he or she is to respond fully to Jesus, benefits immensely by being led and taught by Mary;

— Mary is present within the Church to share her life of response so that the Church may become what she is called to be, learning from Mary's faith, from her humility and love. The Church needs to become Mary-like, needs to become "Marist" — a theme that finds expression in the words of Vatican Council II:

As St Ambrose taught, the mother of God is the model of
the Church in the matter of faith, love and perfect union
with Christ. For in the mystery of the Church, herself
rightly called mother and virgin, the Blessed Virgin
stands out in eminent and singular fashion as exemplar of
both virginity and motherhood. . . .

In the most holy virgin, the Church has already
reached that perfection whereby she exists without spot
or wrinkle. . . the followers of Christ raise their eyes to
Mary who shines forth to the whole community of the
elect as a model of all virtues. Devoutly meditating her...
the Church becomes more like her and continually
progresses in faith, hope and charity, searching out and
doing the will of God in all things.[31]

It is to this — to lead Christians to appreciate Mary's readiness
to share her life of response to the Lord — that Marists are
directed by our tradition's stress on the Mary of the Pentecostal
days.

To be a presence of Mary in the Church today

Against the background of the Church's tradition and present-
day belief, who can doubt that Mary is actively present among
the faithful?

Her being-with-us is highlighted in a particular way by
shrines such as Knock, here in Ireland, or the Lourdes you
have visited in the Pyrenees, or Fatima — places which each
has its history of Mary showing to ordinary country people her
active, loving concern for them, and her continuing presence to
the Church.

Each Marist is to be, in a sense, a living shrine of Mary,
testifying that she is with the Church still, still active in her
work of "bringing Jesus to people" and of "shaping the
disciple's response to the Lord". The Marist is to be "a
presence of Mary to the Church", i.e. what she brought to the
first Christian community, the Marist is to bring to the Church
today; he, or she, is to continue Mary's work, in her spirit,
among the faithful of these present times.

To be a "living shrine of Mary, a living presence of Mary" is
as high-ranking and as noble an ideal as one could reach for. It
can be accepted and striven for from the awareness that Mary
is closely united to her Marists. "She is in our midst", says

175

Colin;[32] she walks with us, she works with us in all that we do.[33]

> "Mary," says Jeanne-Marie Chavoin, "has pledged herself to keep always close to me".[34]

To the founders, Mary is the superior of the Society as she is its foundress;[35] she is the Queen whose banner we follow;[36] she organises, directs, inspires;[37] and the Marist is to let this presence of Mary shine through to others, that they might feel her presence among them. By walking with her, by learning continually from her, by reproducing her way of serving adapted to the context of today's living, we are to bring her presence home to our generation.

So, it is the Marist's life-endeavour to come, more and more,

> to think as Mary thinks,
> to judge as she judges,
> to feel as she feels.
> to act as she would in all things.[38]

Jean Coste, the Marist historian, writes:

> Mary is not a model placed before us towards which we must strive. She is a person whose maternal love has set up special bonds between herself and us, which we have freely ratified. We know her and we love her, and it is a question of remaining so united to her in thought and in heart that our conduct will be enlightened by her presence and will help to perpetuate to some extent that unique manner of living the Christian life that was hers during her life on earth.[39]

Awareness of her being with him leads the Marist to refer naturally to her in prayer, seeking to be open to her guidance, drawing strength from her strength. It is recorded of Champagnat that he confided to Mary all his projects and his works, beginning them only after having long besought her to bless them.[40] And Colin, in a retreat conference, encourages his men:

> We should all make one great resolution — never to say or to do anything without first raising our hearts to Mary, saying: "Blessed Virgin, what must I do? What must I say?"[41]

The natural outcome of this sense of Mary's wish to be with her Christian people, this "Bright White Swan, the first who really cared" as your poet calls her,[42] is that we try to make her known and loved. Champagnat expresses it well:

> . . .to love this noble Queen, to serve her, to spread devotion to her according to the spirit of the Church, as an excellent means of living and serving Jesus Christ easily and more perfectly, such was the aim we had in view in founding the Marist Brothers.[43]

Yet, as I have said, we have no particular practices or devotions that are characteristically Marist; we use whatever means we find at hand, to make Mary known and loved, the practices that are already known and loved by the people, we encourage and develop, — the rosary, the scapular, celebrating Mary's feasts in the liturgy, litanies, novenas, visits to her shrines, wearing her medals, the month of May devotions — whatever is useful in building up a personal relationship between the Blessed Mother and the individual Christian. And that is enough — once the Christian has been brought into contact with Mary and has begun to share life with her, she, active woman, will do the rest. I am reminded of the story that tells of a village where the peasants, desperate for rain, sent for a rain-maker to come and to deliver them from the drought. The rain-maker came — a woman, they were surprised to discover; the villagers waited to witness some impressive ceremony and mighty ritual that would open the stubborn skies. But she quietly took up residence among them and lived with them the ordinary village life. They were perplexed and angry and felt themselves tricked, and disregarded her; but after she had lived with them for a week, soft, steady, soaking rain began to fall. If Mary, "who carries Jesus in her arms and in her heart",[44] dwells with us, this very contact with her will gradually transform Christ's follower, making the Christian, in his or her own turn, a Christ-bringer to others, helping the disciple respond, as Mary did, to the person and message of Jesus.

Summing up

The Marist marian heritage, this gift that enables us to give away the stone, if I might refer back to the story with which I opened this presentation, has been well summed up by

Pope Paul VI who, writing in his apostolic exhortation, *Marialis cultus*, says:

> In the primitive Church
> Mary is seen praying with the apostles;
> in our own day, she is actively present
> and the Church
> wishes to live the mysteries of Christ with her.[45]

The Marist founders must have delighted in his statement, so true is it to their intuitions: Mary, the Mary of Nazareth and of Pentecost, is today *actively present*, the Christ-bringer, the disciple-former, a woman of initiative and daring, wise and determined, yet hidden, unassuming, gentle; and we wish to *live the mysteries of Christ with her*, and to have the Church live the mysteries of Christ with her. To make a Marist contribution to this presence and work of Mary in the hearts of Christ's followers is our privilege, our responsibility and our joy. Mary is the air we breathe as we grow in the Christ-life — and Hopkins beautifully elaborates his:

> I say that we are wound
> with mercy, round and round
> as if with air; the same
> is Mary, more by name.
> She, wild web, wondrous robe. . .
> mantles the guilty globe
> since God has let dispense
> her prayers his providence;
> nay, more than almoner
> the sweet alms' self is her
> and men are meant to share
> her life, as life does air.[46]

Chavoin, Colin, Champagnat and the pioneers of the Marist Missionary Sisters would have appreciated the poet's insight; what he sang of, they lived, and living, passed on to us as the Marist marian heritage.

NOTES AND REFERENCES

Chapter 1: Mary in the New Testament: some thoughts for today

Further reading

J. McHUGH, *The Mother of Jesus in the New Testament.* (London: Darton, Longman and Todd, 1975).

R. E. BROWN, *The Birth of the Messiah: a commentary on the infancy narratives in Matthew and Luke.* (London: Geoffrey Chapman, 1977).

Mary in the New Testament: a Collaborative Assessment by Protestant and Roman Catholic Scholars. Edited by R. E. Brown and others. (London: Geoffrey Chapman, 1978).

Chapter 2: Growth and decline in mariology

1. *Sermones de diversis* 3 in D. Casagrande, *Enchiridion Marianum* — henceforth *EnMar* (Rome: Cor Unum, 1974) n. 325.
2. *EnMar* 519-523.
3. *Canon in dormitionem B.V. Mariae,* 1, *EnMar* 1970.
4. See further M. Saint, *Mary in the Writings of Dante.* "Occasional Papers of the Ecumenical Society of the Blessed Virgin Mary", 1986.
5. See further C. Smith, "Mary in the Theology of Hans Urs von Balthasar" in A. Stacpoole, ed., *Mary and the Churches* (Dublin: Columba, 1987); M. Kehl and W. Löser, eds., *The Von Balthasar Reader* (Edinburgh: Clarke, 1982); H. Urs von Balthasar, *Mary for Today* (Slough: St Paul, 1987); idem., "Die marianische Prägung der Kirche" in W. Beinert, ed., *Maria heute ehren* (Freiburg-Basel-Vienna: Herder, 1977) 263-279.

Bibliography

For history of mariology see:

S. De Fiores and Salvatore Meo, eds., *Nouvo dizionario di mariologia.* (Milan: Ed. Paoline, 1985).

H. Graef, *Mary. A History of Doctrine and Devotion.* 2 vols. (London-New York: Sheed and Ward, 1963).

R. Laurentin, *Court traité de la théologie mariale.* (Paris: 1968) — brief survey.

M. O'Carroll, *Theotokos. A Theological Encyclopedia of the Blessed Virgin Mary.* (Delaware: Glazier-Dublin: Dominican Publications, 1982) — many general and specific articles.

P. O'Dwyer, *Mary. A History of Devotion in Ireland.* (Dublin: Four Courts, 1988).

G. Roschini, *Maria santissima nella storia della salvezza.* 4 vols. (Rome: Ed. Pisani, 1969) — see especially vol. 4.

Chapter 3: The Immaculate Conception and Assumption of Our Lady in today's thinking

1. 603 were consulted: 546 favoured a definition; 4 opposed it; 53 were hesitant on the opportuneness or the mode of presentation.
2. The figures: of 1181 residential bishops, 6 doubted with 16 questioning the opportuneness; of 59 abbots and prelates *nullius,* 2 doubted; of 206 vicars apostolic, 3 doubted; of 381 titular bishops, 5 doubted.
3. A study group composed of five Catholics and five members chosen from the three communions, Church of Ireland, Presbyterian Church and Methodists, was sponsored by the Ballymascanlon Conference. The aim was to report on different attitudes towards Mary among Irish Christians. Five very amicable

meetings took place in the course of 1982 and the report was submitted in January of the following year. Among "problem areas" it identified different attitudes towards the Bible and divine revelation: this would imply different views on the marian privileges, which were not dealt with in detail. These were not explicitly treated either in the ecumenical declarations of the six International Mariological Congresses since the Council (Santo Domingo, Zagreb, Lisbon-Fatima, Rome, Saragossa, Malta). The general differences would of course prevail implicitly.

4.   Discussion of the paper was not extended. The problem of how to communicate truths about Mary to young people was raised. This is a question of the presentation of ideals in personalised form. It is a good thing to remember that young boys are seeking the ideal woman, and young girls can look to Mary as the ideal of their own sex. Paul VI's apostolic exhortation *Marialis cultus* is a helpful source in all matters about imitation of Mary.

Bibliography

All the important papal statements on Mary are in *Papal Teaching*, ed. St Paul, Boston; *Our Lady, Mary: Doctrine and Devotion* by Hilda Graef (London, 2 vols, 1963, 1965) deals with the Immaculate Conception and Assumption at important points in the historical development of the doctrines. M.J. Scheeben, in *Mariology II*, (St Louis, London, 1947) deals extensively with the Immaculate Conception and the Assumption. H.S. Box (Anglican) has articles on the Immaculate Conception and the Assumption in the Anglican symposium, *The Blessed Virgin Mary*, ed. E.L. Mascall and H.S. Box, (London, 1963). Detailed bibliographies are given in the following articles of my own book, *Theotokos*, (Wilmington, Dublin, 1983): *Assumption, Assumption Apocrypha, Immaculate Conception, Ineffabilis Deus, Munificentissimus Deus.* Finally I commend an excellent article by the American mariologist, Fr Eamon Carroll, O Carm, "Papal Infallibility and the Marian definitions. Some Considerations" in *Carmelus*, 26(1979), 213-250.

Chapter 4: Mary in ecumenical dialogue

1.   I owe a debt of thanks for advice offered at draft stage by Rev. John de Satgé (Vice-Principal, Chichester Theological College), Rev. Dr Edward Yarnold, SJ (Senior Tutor, Campion Hall, Oxford) and Rev. and Mrs Geoffrey Pinnock (ESBVM).

2.   Vatican II Decree *Dei Verbum*, n. 8.

3.   Michael O'Carroll, CSSp, 'Mary as Revelation', *Marianum* 44 (1982), 282-3.

4.   Vatican Decree on Ecumenism, n. 13: as a result of the Reformation many Communions were separated from the See of Rome: "Among those in which some Catholic traditions and institutions continue to exist, the Anglican Communion occupies a special place."

5.   Leading figures from the French Church included Yves Congar, OP, Jean Daniélou, SJ, and Henri de Lubac, SJ, (both subsequently promoted Cardinals); from the German Church, the Jesuit brothers Hugo and Karl Rahner, the excitable Tübingen theologian Hans Küng, and perhaps we should add Josef Ratzinger since he is now the Cardinal Prefect of the Sacred Congregation for the Doctrine of the Faith.

6.   Such consciousness centres especially around ICEL for the liturgy, and ARCIC for ecumenical theology issuing in bi-lateral Agreed Statements. From Canada comes arguably the most brilliant ecumenist of our time, a French Dominican Père Jean-Marie Tillard of the Dominican Faculty of Theology, Ottawa.

7.   Cf. Michael O'Carroll, CSSp, "Ecumenism and Our Lady: the English

Notes and references

situation", *Ephemerides Mariologicae* (1983), 193-323, esp 293f.

8. Alberic Stacpoole, OSB, "The English Tradition of the Doctrine of the Immaculate Conception," in A. J. Stacpoole ed., *Mary's Place in Christian dialogue* (1982), 217-31. (In the English version on p. 228 is a displacement of print, corrected in the American version: the tenth line paragraph should follow the second line.)

9. Cf. Ralph Townsend, "The Place of Mary in Early Anglican Thought", ESBVM paper (May 1983), 1-8.

10. Ed. F.E. Hutchinson, *The Works of George Herbert* (Oxford, 1941, revised 1959), 78; G.K. Studdert-Kennedy, *The Unutterable Beauty* (London: Hodder & Stoughton, 1947; Mowbray, 1983), 98.

11. *Letters and Diaries* XII, 153f.

12. *Parochial & Plain Sermons* II. 131f.

13. Cf. L. Govaert, "Our Lady in the Thought and Devotion of the Anglican Newman", *Ampleforth Review* (Spring 1979), 20-30; this, as Editor, I was able to commission from her work for a doctoral thesis, *Kardinal Newmans Mariologie und sein persönlicher Werdegang,* Salzburg, 1975. She is now the Rome secretary of the Friends of Cardinal Newman. Cf. also Roderick Strange, "The development of Newman's marian thought and devotion," *One in Christ* 1980-1/2, 114-26 (ESBVM reprint, 61-73), which does not show development (because the author, whose D. Phil concerned Newman, finds him "massively consistent" and therefore provides only five dates in the paper) but analysis: Mary as second Eve, as immaculately conceived, as mother, as assumed into heaven. Cf. also Charles Stephen Dessain, "Cardinal Newman's Teaching about the Blessed Virgin Mary", in A.J. Stacpoole ed., *Mary's Place in Christian dialogue* (1982) 232-47.

14. "And if we take a survey at least of Europe, we shall find that it is not those religious communions which are characterised by devotion towards the Blessed Virgin that have ceased to adore her Eternal Son, but those very bodies, which have renounced devotion to her . . . they who were accused of worshipping a creature in his stead, still worship him; their accusers who hoped to worship him so purely . . . have ceased to worship him altogether." *Essay on Development* (1845/1879), 426.

15. *Parochial & Plain Sermons* II. 31.

16. Pius XII, *Discorsi e radiomessaggi di Sua Santita Pio XII,* XIV 2 ed, Citta del Vaticano (1953), 130; quoting Newman's *Discourses to mixed congregations* XVII, 348. The text, more fully, is this: "If Mary is the mother of God, Christ must be literally Emmanuel, God with us. And hence it was that, when time went on, and the bad spirits and false prophets grew stronger and bolder, and found a way into the Catholic body itself, then the Church, guided by God, could find no more effectual and sure way of expelling them than that of using this word *Deipara* against them; and, on the other hand, when (they plotted again in the sixteenth century) they could find no more certain expedient for their hateful purpose than that of reviling and blaspheming the prerogatives of Mary; for they knew full well that, if they could only get the world to dishonour the mother, the dishonour of the son would follow close. The Church and Satan agreed together in this, that son and mother went together, and the experience of three centuries has confirmed their testimony, for Catholics who have honoured the mother, still worship the son, while Protestants, who now have ceased to confess the son, began by scoffing at the mother."

17. Donal Flanagan, "An Ecumenical Future for Roman Catholic Theology of Mary", in A.J. Stacpoole ed., *Mary's place in Christian dialogue* (1982), 3-24.

18. E. Hoskyns, "Genesis 1-3 and St John's Gospel", JTS 31 (1920), 221.

19. E. Hoskyns, *The Fourth Gospel* (2nd ed, F.N. Davey, 1950), 530.

20. In his diocesan leaflet prior to the Vatican Council, one English bishop had written: "It is my personal hope that the Holy Father will see fit to crown our love of our glorious and Blessed Mother, Queen of Heaven and Ever Virgin, with the definition of the dogmas of Maria Mediatrix and Maria fons gratiae, which have been in the prayers and devotions of the faithful."

21. Dom Edmund Carruth, *Mary and the Council* (1969). Cf. S. Napiokowski, "The Present Position in Mariology", *Concilium* 9/3 (1967), 52-62, which makes a distinction between a christotypical and an ecclesiotypical mariology (i.e. ordered back to her Son, or ordered forward to the Church).

22. *Lumen Gentium* VII 5, n. 69. Most translations are unsatisfactory.

23. Downside Abbey Archives: a series of letters were sent from Rome to the Prior, and then made available to the other Abbeys of the Congregation.

24. Ms in A.J.S. files. The Abbé Laurentin of Angers, a leading international mariologist, speaks regularly at the Congresses of the ESBVM.

25. Its complete distilled deliberations are published in *The Final Report* (CTS/SPCK 1982), covering all its publications during 1972-82. Appendices give detailed lists of the Commission's meetings and members. For convenience, the Joint Preparatory Commission's "Malta Report" of 1968 is also there published.

26. H. Bettenson, *Documents of the Christian Church* (2 ed, Oxford, 1967), 327-9. Addressed "to all Christian people", it is an appeal for Reunion.

27. Common Declaration, 24 March 1966, *Final Report*, 117f.

28. Common Declaration, 29 April 1977, *Final Report*, 119-22.

29. Common Declaration, 29 March 1982, *The Pope teaches* (CTS, 1982); *The Pope in Britain: all the speeches and homilies* (St Paul Publications, 1982); Peter Jennings, *The Pope in Britain* (Bodley Head, 1982).

30. (Bishop) Alan C. Clark and Colin Davey, *Anglican/Roman Catholic Dialogue; the Work of the Preparatory Commission* (Oxford, 1974).

31. *Final Report*, 95-6.

32. ARCIC 18, paper VII (unpublished), Lambeth Library.

33. Examples from the Catholic side are Hugo Rahner, SJ, *Our Lady & the Church* (DLT, 1962) and Karl Rahner, SJ, *Mary, Mother of the Lord* (Nelson, 1962); from the Anglican side, Edd E. Mascall and H.S. Box, *The Blessed Virgin Mary* (1963), which includes essays by A.M. Allchin, A. Farrer, Dom A. Morris, J. de Satgé, J.C. Stephenson and E. Symonds.

34. ARCIC 116; *One in Christ* (1975-6), 2.29, esp 5-7, 25, and footnotes.

35. *Final Report*, 96 note 6. The footnote was drafted by Rev. Howard Root with Fr George Tavard: it is argued that when one Church's point of view is being explained, it is so done out of the main text.

36. Edward Yarnold, SJ, "Anglicans, Roman Catholics and the Blessed Virgin Mary", the third Martin Gillett Memorial Lecture, ESBVM, March 1982, 1-7, republished in *One in Christ*, (1983), 274-80. He quotes an earlier ESBVM paper (*vide supra*, note 17) which described these marian dogmas as "truths about the nature of Christian salvation, as salvation in and through Christ and his community, not just doctrinal information about Mary. They represent, in theological terms, not embarrassing pietism posing as theology but true gains in the field of the doctrines of Christian anthropology and eschatology which we ignore to our loss." (p. 18 in ESBVM pamphlet, p. 18f in A.J. Stacpoole, ed., *Mary's Place in Christian dialogue*).

37. That is the current wording of the Society's aims, it having been honed down at successive council meetings. The Society is fond of stating that it has three aspects to its activities: study, prayer and fellowship, two of these being invoked at any one meeting.

38. A.J. Stacpoole, "International Ecumenical Conference: ESBVM", *Ampleforth*

Journal (Summer 1973), 64-73. The Laurentin paper was later issued as a pamphlet, by ESBVM.

39. A.J. Stacpoole, "The Third International Ecumenical Conference: ESBVM", *Ampleforth Journal* (Autumn 1975), 23-30; ibid. (Spring 1976), 33-9. Cf. John Mc Hugh, "Exegesis & Dogma: a Review of Two Marian studies", with a reply by Rev. Professor Raymond E. Brown, SS, *Ampleforth Review* (1980), 43-61. Cf. also John McHugh, *The Mother of Jesus in the New Testament* (DLT, 1975).

40. *One in Christ* 1980-1/2, 54-154. This Catholic ecumenical quarterly, which continues the work of the *Eastern Churches Quarterly* and others, seeks to further the movement towards Christian unity by giving information on topics of ecumenical concern, by contributing to the dialogue between Christians, and by encouraging love between Christians and prayer for Christian unity. Over the years it has given coverage to the work of ESBVM on several occasions.

41. The last two congresses, since the death of Martin Gillett, have been organised by the General Secretary, Dom Alberic Stacpoole, with committees at Canterbury and Dublin, as well as the Council which meets three times a year (the autumn meeting being in the Jerusalem Chamber, Westminster Abbey).

42. Cardinal Suenens' letter of July 1983 reads: "My role will be to pray for your precious ecumenical work, and to ask from time to time our dear Martin Gillett in heaven to help you on the road."

43. A.J. Stacpoole, OSB, "The Recent Work of ESBVM, 1980-84", *One in Christ,* 1980-83, 262-8; it is followed by two of the Society's occasional papers, the first by Fr Yarnold (*supra*), the second by another ARCIC member, now the Archdeacon of Westminster, Bishop Edward Knapp-Fisher, "Prospects for Unity: an Anglican View".

44. Alberic Stacpoole, OSB, ed., *Mary's Place in Christian Dialogue* (St Paul Publications, 281p, 1982). It includes a paper given by an early patron, the then Apostolic Delegate, Archbishop H.E. Cardinale (d. 1983 aged 66) in Central Hall, Westminster in March 1969. "Pope Pius XII and the Blessed Virgin Mary".

45. "To all bishops in peace and communion with the Apostolic See, for the right ordering and development of devotion to the Blessed Virgin Mary."

46. Ed. Raymond E. Brown, Karl P. Donfried, Joseph A. Fitzmyer, John Reumann. *Mary in the New Testament* (Chapman, 1978); Cf. John McHugh, *The Mother of Jesus in the New Testament* (DLT, 1975), and art. cit. in note 39 above.

47. Ibid 6, "Origins of the Study".

48. Text and discussion in Frederick M. Jelly, OP, "Mary's Intercession: a Contemporary Reappraisal", *Marian Studies* XXXII (1981), 76-95, esp 76. Fr Jelly is a member of ESBVM, from Columbus, Ohio.

49. It has, however, been argued that the discipline of proper connection with the *magisterium ecclesiae* is present in the fact that this was the ninth mariological (i.e. scientific, as contrasted with "marian", which is devotional) congress of the Pontificia Academia Mariana Internationale, whose *praeses* is Padre Paulus Melada, OFM, and whose address is Via Merulana 124, 00185 Roma. The Padre and his colleagues are for the most part Croatian. PAMI, a papal foundation, has a tradition of serious ecumenical concern. The question remains: does it have a valid control over the Congress its administrators convene, or do the deliberations of the independent guest-scholars go beyond what PAMI may choose to underwrite? And again: is PAMI authorised, by its constitution, to underwrite ecumenical declarations, as an official agent of the *magisterium*?

50. Source as yet unprinted (except in the *ESBVM Newsletter* No. 25, January 1984, 4-5, introduced by John de Satgé) signed by seven Catholics led by Eamon Carroll, O Carm, (also ESBVM), four Anglicans led by John de Satgé (also ESBVM), one Orthodox, one Lutheran, and one Reformed (a balance of 7 Catholic, 7 non-Catholic.)

Mary in the Church

Chapter 7: Mary and women

1. D. Flanagan, *In Praise of Mary* (Dublin: Veritas, 1975) 99.
2. "Sexism and God-Talk" in *Women and Men: the Consequences of Power* (Cincinnati, 1976) 421.
3. M. Kilbenshlag, *Goodbye Sleeping Beauty* (Dublin: Arlen House, 1983) 201.
4. *Dives in misericordia* ("On Divine Mercy") 4, n. 52 (London: CTS, 1980) 21.
5. See C. O'Donnell, "Mary, the True Disciple" in P. Rogers, ed., *Sowing the Word* (Dublin: Dominican Publications, 1983) 230-237.
6. See E. Moltmann-Wendel, *The Women Around Jesus* (London: SCM, 1982) 81-90.
7. See S.M. Schneider, "Women in the Fourth Gospel and the Role of Women in the Contemporary Church", *Bible Theology Bulletin* 12 (1982) 41.

Bibliography

I. Brennan, "Women in the Kingdom" *Jesus Caritas* 61 (1983) 5—10.

R. Brown, K. P. Donfried, J. A. Fitzmyer, J. Reumann eds., *Mary in the New Testament* (London: Chapman, 1978).

M. Carroll, *Theotokos*. (Wilmington, Delaware: Glazier, 1982).

H. Concannon, *The Queen of Ireland* (Dublin: Gill, 1938).

A. Emery, "On Devotion to Mary" *New Covenant* 11 (1982) 12—14.

D. Flanagan, *In Praise of Mary* (Dublin: Veritas, 1975).

H. Graef, *Mary: A History of Doctrine and Devotion.* 2 vols. (London: Sheed and Ward, 1963).

M. Kilbenshlag, *Goodbye Sleeping Beauty* (Dublin: Arlen House, 1983).

H. Küng and J. Moltmann (eds.) "Mary in the Churches", *Concilium* 168 (1983)

E. Moltmann-Wendel, *The Women Around Jesus* (London: SCM, 1982).

C. O'Donnell, "Mary the True Disciple" in, P. Rogers, ed., *Sowing the Word.* (Dublin: Dominican Publications, 1983), 230—237.

P. Ó Duibhir, "An Mhaighdean Mhuire agus an Nua-Spriodáltacht" in M. Mac Conmara, ed., *An Léann Eaglasta 1000-1200* (Dublin: An Clóchomar, 1982), 70—76.

P. O'Dwyer, Mary. *A History of Devotion in Ireland* (Dublin: Four Courts, 1988).

Pope John Paul, *Dives in misericordia*, (London: CTS, 1980).

Pope Paul VI, *Marialis cultus.* (Athlone. St Paul Publication, 1974).

R. Ruether, "Sexism and God-Talk" in *Women and Men: the Consequences of Power* (Cincinnati: 1976).

S. M. Schneider, "The Effects of Women's Experience on Their Spirituality", *Spirituality Today* 35 (1983) 100—116.

S. M. Schneider, "Women in the Fourth Gospel and the Role of Women in the Contemporary Church", *Bible Theology Bulletin* 12 (1982) 35—45.

A. Stacpoole, ed., *Mary's Place in Christian Dialogue* (Slough: St Paul Publication, 1982).

Chapter 8: The impact of feminism on mariology

Further Reading

C. Halkes, "Mary and Women" and K. Borresen, "Mary in Catholic Theology", both in *Concilium* 168(1983), an issue devoted to "Mary in the Churches".

Notes and references

Chapter 9: Mary and youth today

1. E. Voegelin, "Immortality: Symbol and Experience". *Harvard Theological Review*, (1967).
2. C. O'Donnell, *Life in the Spirit and Mary*. (Wiimington: Glazier — Dublin: Dominican Publications, 1981) 11.
3. Pope Paul VI, *To Honour Mary – Marialis cultus* (London: CTS, 1974) n. 17.
4. Vatican II, Liturgy Constitution, n. 103.
5. R. M. Reuther, *The Feminine Face of the Church,* (London: SCM Press, 1979).
6. C. O'Donnell, op. cit. 100.
7. Pope Paul VI, *Marialis cultus*, n. 37.

Chapter 12: Mary in the Irish tradition

1. M.A. O'Brien, "The Old Irish Life of St Brigit" *Irish Historical Studies* I, 1938-9, 348.
2. Peter O'Dwyer, O Carm, *A Fresh Look at Versiculi Familiae Benchuir,* Carmelite Publications (Dublin: 1975) 2-13.
3. James Carney, *The Poems of Blathmac son of Cú Brettan together with the Irish Gospel of St Thomas and a Poem on the Virgin Mary* (Dublin, 1964). These are references which had a special appeal for me.
4. J.H. Bernard and R. Atkinson, *The Irish Liber Hymnorum* I, 32-4.
5. Whitley Stokes, *The Martyrology of Oengus the Culdee* (London, 1905) and R.I. Best and H.J. Lawlor, *The Martyrology of Tallaght* (London, 1931) see under dates 3 May, 6 July, 14 December.
6. Françoise Henry, *Irish Art during the Viking Invasions* (London, 1967) 69, 78-9, 188.
7. A. Gwynn and R.N. Hadcock, *Medieval Religious Houses in Ireland* (London, 1979) *passim.*
8. E.J. Gwynn and W. Purton, "The Monastery of Tallaght" in *Proceedings of the Royal Irish Academy* XXIX, Sect. C, 127. v. also *Liber Hymnorum* I, 53.
9. B. Ó Cúiv, *Ériu* XIX, 13-7.
10. Gerard Murphy, *Early Irish Lyrics,* (Oxford, 1956) 46-51.
11. Charles Donahue, *The Testament of Mary* (New York, 1942) 27.
12. *Early Irish Lyrics* 51.
13. Fr McKenna in his introduction to *Dán Dé* (v.n. 15) and *Philip Bocht* (v.n. 28) gives a systematic list of references to dogmatic truths and points of interest regarding Mary which are found in Bardic poems.
14. C. Plummer, *Irish Litanies* (London, 1925) 48-51.
15. He is a thirteenth century poet and many poems are attributed to him. Very probably he was not the author of them all but I use them to reflect the Irish mind of the times. His poetry is edited by L. McKenna, *Dán Dé* (Dublin, 1922).
16. Ibid., *Mairg nach tathaigh na trátha* (stt. 21-5).
17. Ibid., Poem XXVI, st. 44.
18. Ibid., Poem XXVII, stt. 34-5.
19. Tomás Ó Máille, *Archivium Hibernicum* II, 256-73.
20. L. McKenna, SJ, *An Timthire* 1918, 51-2.
21. Osborn Bergin, *Irish Bardic Poetry* (Dublin, 1970) Poem 21.
22. L. McKenna, *Aithdioghluim Dána* (Dublin, 1939-40) henceforth *Aith. D.,* Poem 49.
23. B. Ó Cúiv, "A Poem on the Infancy of Christ", *Éigse* XV, 93-102.
24. *Aith D.,* Poem 69 st. 23.
25. *Dán Dé,* Poem VII stt. 31-2.

26. Ibid., Poem XV st. 3.
27. v. *Celtica* VI, 82 and VII, 163-87.
28. L. McKenna, *Philip Bocht Ó Huiginn* (Dublin, 1931).
29. Ibid., Poem II st. 36.
30. Ibid., Poem IV st. 35.
31. Ibid., Poem VI stt. 4-5.
32. Ibid., Poem IX st. 18.
33. Ibid., stt. 20-1.
34. Ibid., st. 32.
35. Ibid., Poem XI(a).
36. Ibid., Poem XXI, stt. 26-30.
37. J. O'Donovan, *The Annals of the Four Masters* (Dublin, 1851) 1397, 1412.
38. M. MacNamara, MSC, *The Apocrypha in the Irish Church* (Dublin 1975), 4.
39. Cainneach Ó Maonaigh, *Smaointe Beatha Chríost* (Dublin, 1944).
40. Brussels MS 20978-9 (Bibliothèque Nationale).
41. L. McKenna, SJ, *Dánta do chum Aonghus Fionn Ó Dálaigh* (Dublin, 1919) (henceforth *AF*) Poem 30 st. 28.
42. *Aith. D.,* Poem 60, stt. 8-11.
43. Ibid., Poem 72.
44. Ibid., Poem 93, st. 9.
45. *AF*, iv.
46. Ibid., Poem 9.
47. Ibid., Poem 10 st. 7.
48. Ibid., Poem 12 st. 3.
49. Ibid., Poem 26 st. 10.
50. L. McKenna, SJ, *Dioghluim Dána* (Dublin, 1938, henceforth *Di. D.*), Poem 19.
51. E. Hogan, SJ, *Ibernia Ignatiana* I App. 232. Rev. Paul Walsh, *Beatha Aodha Ruaidh Mhic Domhnaill* (London, 1957) 224-5. Helena Concannon, *The Queen of Ireland* (Dublin, 1938) 130.
52. *Aith D.* Poem 85, st. 10.
53. Alice Curtayne, *St Patrick's Purgatory* (Monaghan, 1962) 52-3.
54. *Di. D.* Poem No 48, st. 26.
55. Peter O'Dwyer, O Carm, *Highlights in Devotion to Mary in Ireland from 1600* (Dublin, 1981) (henceforth *Highlights*), 20-3.
56. Royal Irish Academy MS. G vi I, 89.
57. Pádraig Ó Canainn *Filídheacht na nGaedheal* (Dublin, 1940) 25-1.
58. Nuala Costello, "Two Diaries of the French Expedition 1798", *Analecta Hibernica* XI, 64-7, 89, 122.
59. *Highlights*, 70-3.
60. Royal Irish Academy, MS 23 C 20, 175-6.
61. *Highlights*, 78-80.
62. Ibid 82-4.
63. Enrí Ó Muirgheasa, *Dánta Diadha Uladh* (Dublin, 1936) Poem I st. 12.
64. *Highlights* 91.
65. Diarmuid Ó Laoghaire, SJ, *Ár bPaidreacha Dúchais* (Dublin, 1975).
66. Joseph Cunnane, "The Doctrinal Content of Irish Marian Piety", *Mother of the Redeemer*, ed. Kevin McNamara (Dublin, 1959), 286.
67. While this article was in proof, the volume *Mary: A History of Irish Devotion* (Four Courts Press, 1988) by Peter O'Dwyer, O Carm, has been published.

Chapter 13: Marist marian heritage

1. Anthony de Mello, *The Song of the Bird*, (Gujarat Sahitya Prakash, Anand, India, 1982) 182-183.

2. J. Coste, SM, and G. Lessard, SM, *Origines Maristes* (Rome: Tipografia Pio X, 1961) doc. 718, 5.

3. "...Jesus and Mary dwell in hearts open to them. Involve Mary in all you do", Champagnat, letter to Br Antoine, 4 February 1831.

4. "(the Society) is the work of the Blessed Virgin", Chavoin, *Correspondence/Recollections of Mother St Joseph,* (Rome 1966/1974), hereafter referred to as *CR,* doc. 107;1.

   "this (Society) is your work, Mary", Champagnat, *Life of Father Champagnat,* (Tournai: Desclée, 1947), hereafter referred to as *Life,* p. 96.

   "Mary is the foundress of the Society", Colin, *The Founder Speaks,* (Rome, 1975), hereafter referred to as *FS,* doc. 143;10.

5. "What gratitude we should show Mary for having chosen us to spread her Society", Colin, *FS,* doc. 78; 2.

   "Think how Mary has loved you and chosen you. . .to be one of her own", Chavoin, *CR,* doc. 87; 2.

   "This good Mother has chosen you and set you apart from the world", Champagnat, Circular of 15 August 1837, Circs. I, p. 15.

6. "The Blessed Virgin is our Mistress; she is our Queen. . .I am the staff in her hand; she holds the staff. . .she runs everything", Colin, *FS,* doc. 46; 2-3.

   "Mary has charge of us, being our Mother, Patroness, Superioress. . . this Society is her work", Champagnat, *Life,* p. 365.

7. Cf. Vatican II, *Lumen Gentium,* 62, 65; Paul VI, *Marialis cultus,* 11, 16, 26.

8. Fr Eamon Mac Craoidhe, OSM, *Queen of the Bright Light* (Servite Publications, Ireland, 1983) , 4.

9. Cf. Lk 2:52.

10. Luke 1:38.

11. Colin, *FS,* doc. 60; 1.

12. Joseph Campbell, *Poems,* ed. Austin Clarke (Dublin: Figgis, 1963) 25.

13. Ibid. 40-41.

14. Caryll Houslander, "The Reed" in F.J. Sheed, ed., *The Mary Book* (New York: Sheed and Ward, 1951) 206.

15. Champagnat, *Life* 353, 535.

16. Colin, *FS,* doc, 44; 7.

17. Champagnat, *Life* 107; cf. Chavoin, "Each member of the Society must set herself to live the life of this divine Mother, which is nothing else than the life of Jesus Christ", *CR,* doc. 18; 1.

18. Colin, *FS,* doc. 143; 2.

19. Chavoin, *CR,* doc. 241; 152. Cf. Colin, *FS,* doc. 85; 2: 190; 2-3. Cf. S. Marie de la Croix, SMSM pioneer writing 5 July 1861: "Our vocation is to be unknown, hidden in God. Our zeal, the quiet zeal of Mary without fuss, sometimes not understanding anything ourselves, it is all done so quietly. Our silence should be the silence of Mary's heart, but deep down, that fire which burns before God in secret".

20. Colin, *FS* doc. 116; 8: "Let us imitate our Mother; she did not have people speak of her — the gospel names her only four times — and yet what good she did! . . . let us have her spirit, let us do good hidden and unknown in the eyes of the world. May the world not know of our works; the eye of God will see them and reward them".

21. Fr Eamon Mac Craoidhe, *Queen of the Bright Light,* (Servite Publications, Ireland, 1983) 20.

22. Colin, *FS,* doc. 190; 2-3.

23. Gerard Manley Hopkins, *Selected Poems* edited by James Reeves (London: Heinemann, 1961): 58-59 — "The Blessed Virgin Compared to the Air we Breathe".

24. Luke, Acts 1: 12-14.
25. Colin, *Origines Maristes,* doc. 422; cf. docs. 582, 631, 674, 752; 43.
26. Colin, *FS*, docs. 141; 18: 160: 7.
27. Paul VI, *Marialis cultus*, 37.
28. Paul VI, *Marialis cultus*, 21.
29. Colin, *FS*, doc. 1; 1. Cf. Champagnat: "Every diocese in the world comes within our scope", Letter to Bishop of Grenoble, 15 February 1837.
30. Colin, *FS,* doc. 189; 2.
31. Vatican Council II, *Lumen gentium*, n 63-65.
32. Colin, *FS,* doc. 141; 2.
33. Champagnat, *Life*, pp. 95-96.
34. Chavoin, *CR*, doc. 97; 9.
35. Champagnat, *Life,* p. 551.
36. Champagnat, Circ. of 12 August 1837, Circs. I., p. 14. Colin, *FS*, doc. 46; 1.
37. Chavoin, *CR*, doc. 15; 1.
38. Colin, Circular 1, April, 1842. Cf. J. Coste, *The Spirit of the Society*, Rome, 1963, p. 624.
39. J. Coste, SM, *The Spirit of the Society*, 656.
40. Champagnat, *Life*, 355.
41. Colin, *FS*, doc. 141; 2.
42. Fr Eamon Mac Craoidhe, OSM, *Queen of the Bright Light*, 25.
43. Champagnat, *Life*, 359.
44. Champagnat, letter to Bishop Pompallier, 27 May 1838.
45. Paul VI, *Marialis cultus*, 11.
46. G.M. Hopkins, "The Blessed Virgin compared to the Air we Breathe," *Selected Poems* (London: Heinemann, 1961), 58.

REAPERS OF THE HARVEST

The Redemptorists in Great Britain and Ireland, 1843-98

John Sharp

This is not merely a book for the student of Church history. It is a vivid and fascinating account of a colourful and, at times, controversial body of men who, in the face of opposition from local secular churchmen, soon established themselves as important members of the apostolate in Ireland and the United Kingdom.

Fr John Sharp's highly readable book is the fruit of extensive research in Roman, English, Scottish and Irish archives. His findings constitute a historical work of considerable importance.

£30   320 pp   Hardback

Available from
Veritas, 7-8 Lower Abbey Street, Dublin 1.
Also from Veritas shops in Stillorgan, Cork, Ennis, Letterkenny and Sligo and from Veritas Book and Video Distribution Ltd, Leamington Spa.

ALONE WITH GOD

THIRTY EUCHARISTIC MEDITATIONS

Jean Beyer SJ
Translated from the French by Sr Áine Hayde

These incomparable, scripturally based reflections – hitherto published privately and anonymously – form an inspiring prayer companion.

Each prayer is centred on a divine mystery and designed to facilitate the prayer of simplicity. The short line, blank verse format makes for ease of reading and facilitates assimilation of each thought.

£4.95   113pp   Paperback

Available from
Veritas, 7-8 Lower Abbey Street, Dublin 1.

Also from Veritas shops in Stillorgan, Cork, Ennis, Letterkenny and Sligo and from Veritas Book and Video Distribution Ltd, Leamington Spa.

THE VERITAS BOOK OF BLESSING PRAYERS

The Veritas Book of Blessing Prayers covers just about every conceivable situation that a priest, deacon or any other minister is likely to encounter in our space age consumer society. It offers blessings for such sad situations as addiction, bereavement by suicide, and for children of separated parents, deserted wives.

There are also those frequently requested prayers and readings for spiritual, mental and physical healing.

Happily, the readings and prayers for situations of hope and joy outweigh those for sad ones. They include the blessing of the Advent wreath, Christmas candles, the Christmas crib, lay ministers, missionaries, pilgrims, on the occasion of wedding anniversaries, for world peace.

There are prayers, readings and a blessing too for animals including both farm stock and domestic pets.

The Veritas Book of Blessing Prayers makes a most useful addition to the bookshelf not alone of priests but of all Christians who are charged with the care of a family or called to pray for and with others in times of distress and of celebration.

£8.50   Paperback   214 pp

Available from
Veritas, 7-8 Lower Abbey Street, Dublin 1.

Also from Veritas shops in Stillorgan, Cork, Ennis, Letterkenny and Sligo
and from Veritas Book and Video Distribution Ltd, Leamington Spa.

THE APPARITIONS OF OUR LADY

René Laurentin

An authoritative analysis of reported apparitions of Our Lady by René Laurentin, the Church's most eminent marian theologian. Fr Laurentin helps chart a safe course between the extremes of naive credulity or illuminism on the one hand and outright rejection on the other. The book offers useful insights into the Church's attitude to such phenomena.

Fr Laurentin has rigorously examined an astonishing number of alleged apparitions from Central America to the Far East. His scholarly on-the-spot investigations begin at Finca Betania in Venezuela where the apparitions have recently been officially recognised by the Church – a milestone, considering the rigorous criteria which are applied to 'the supernatural made visible' before such pronouncements are made. By contrast he cites cases which did not meet the criteria, such as Garabandal. Such rejections, he explains, do not necessarily reflect on the integrity or sincerity of the people involved.

£7.95   160pp Paperback

Available from
Veritas , 7-8 Lower Abbey Street, Dublin 1.

Also from Veritas shops in Stillorgan, Cork, Ennis, Letterkenny and Sligo and from Veritas Book and Video Distribution Ltd, Leamington Spa.